Writing Winning Proposals

Judith Mirick Gooch

D1194536

Council for Advancement and Support of Education

ISBN 0-89964-249-7

Printed in the United States of America.

The Council for Advancement and Support of Education (CASE) provides books, art packages, microfiche, and focus issues of the monthly magazine, CURRENTS, for professionals in institutional advancement. The books cover topics in alumni administration, creative communications, fund raising, government relations, institutional relations, management, publications, and student recruitment. For a copy of the catalog, RESOURCES, write to the CASE Publications Order Department, 80 South Early Street, Alexandria, VA 22304.

Book design by Richard Rabil
Cover illustration by Michael David Brown

Council for Advancement and Support of Education
Suite 400, 11 Dupont Circle, Washington, DC 20036

Contents

Letter from the President

Grantsmanship has received its share of opprobrium in recent years as most colleges and universities, suffering from cutbacks in federal money and ever-increasing costs, are turning to corporations and foundations for funding. This criticism is deserved when instead of developing funding to match its programs, an institution attempts to develop programs to match the funding. On the other hand, the proposal writer who believes that any corporation or foundation would be glad to support any program of his or her institution is in for some big disappointments.

In *Writing Winning Proposals,* Judy Gooch cautions us, "No matter how convincing your statistics, how strong your institution, how eloquent your prose, or how well your president knows the chair of their board, you're only going to get the grant if it's for a purpose that the donor finds appealing."

It is no accident that the first chapter in this book is the chapter on research. You cannot approach an organization successfully until you have discovered that special area where your institution's interests and that of the corporation or foundation overlap. A corporation that only supports building projects or major pieces of equipment is not going to fund your chair in Oriental Art. Nor will it serve your institution or the potential grant-maker if you decide that what your institution needs is a new Fine Arts wing when you have declining arts enrollments and empty space in the Cultural Center completed a few years ago.

Gooch never lets us forget that it is not the proposal writer's job merely to seek money. We would all agree that a proposal writer who brings no money to his or her institution should seek a new line of work. But less obvious is the fact that the proposal writer who brings money to the institution—but all for the wrong projects—is just as much a failure in the long run. The institution that allows its vision to be distorted, that molds and shapes its projects and programs according to the availability of corporate and foundation funds, is in deep trouble. It may find itself committed to programs that are inappropriate in the context of its mission, and for which the original funding was insufficient. It may find itself going in directions completely antithetical to its traditional goals.

Integrity is the answer: "To thine own self be true" the magic formula. You must never forget that the funding must serve your institution's mission, and not the other way around.

To Judy Gooch, the proposal writer's task is one of maintaining and sharing the institution's vision and making that vision clear to the individuals who control foundation and corporate resources. We are grateful to her for reminding us that for the proposal writer, as for other advancement professionals, being true to the ideals and missions of his or her institution is a first priority.

Gary H. Quehl
President, CASE
January 1987

Foreword

I remember once reading a commentary on "of course" knowledge. The author's thesis was that there are areas of knowledge that when presented clearly are likely to elicit an "of course" response from the reader. The presentation seems to state, perhaps in more elegant or succinct terms, what we knew already. And so we frequently respond, "That is obvious to any intelligent person," or "Of course."

The author then went on to say that often what appears to be the presentation of common knowledge really is not. The reader has been fooled into thinking that he or she already knew it because the new information fit so neatly into the structure of present knowledge.

Much of the most important learning in life involves unconscious, incidental learning. We often find that we are able to do something that we could not previously do, or that we have come to know something that we cannot recall learning. We can learn without realizing that we are learning, and be taught without giving credit to the teacher. But we also can fail to learn that which is presented to us for our instruction.

The problem with "of course" information is that we may quickly read past that which we think we know, missing the chance to truly learn it. When we need to change the way we act because of what we have learned, it is good to mark that learning with conscious recognition that something has changed. An aphorism to remember is: It is hard to learn that which you already "know."

How then can an author convey "of course" knowledge? There are two ways to deal with the problem of presenting such information. The author can translate the presentation into jargon and neologisms to catch the reader's attention and force more careful reading. Giving ideas new labels may make the reader believe that he or she is learning something new. Treatises in sociology, psychology, and management regularly use this device.

But there is another way: The author can present the problem to the reader and invite the reader to state what he or she knows about the subject. This makes it harder for the reader to pass over the material, claiming, "I knew that already." Thus, when he or she gets the "of course" feeling, it may mean, "That makes sense," or "Why didn't I think of that?"

Much, if not most, of the writing about how to do fund raising falls into the category of "of course" knowledge. I don't mean to suggest that all such writing represents new and profound information previously unknown to the reader. There is as much banality in writing on development as there is in any other field.

But because writing about fund raising often contains so much "of course" knowledge, we need to read more carefully and critically, sorting out what we need to know from what is not worth knowing, but is presented in an engaging manner.

In this book, Judy Gooch presents her material straightforwardly, without jargon. This means there is a significant danger that you may read some of the text as "of course" knowledge. Let me caution you not to be misled into missing significant pieces of useful information because she has written so clearly and so matter-of-factly. I urge you to test your own knowledge against hers before you begin reading *Writing Winning Proposals*. In this way, you will reap the full benefit of her wisdom and experience.

Richard R. Johnson
Research Director
Exxon Education Foundation

Introduction

In the spring of 1982, Deborah J. Cohen, director of communications at Massachusetts Institute of Technology, asked if I would work with her to design and teach a workshop for new development officers whose portfolios included writing requests for corporate and foundation support. Most people involved in this relatively new area of educational fund raising had learned to write proposals, as Debbie and I had learned, by doing it. Unlike other advancement professionals, proposal writers from different institutions didn't get together much. Although a few organizations offered courses in grant writing, most focused on preparing proposals for government agencies, and none was designed specifically for people in education, writing proposals for foundations and corporations.

The first CASE Writing Winning Proposals Workshop was an instant sell-out; it has been offered twice each year since 1982 and has spun off a subsidiary for those writing proposals for elementary and secondary schools. Faculty have included, besides Debbie and me, James H. Frey of Kent Place School, Andrew J. Grant of Hofstra University, Sarah C. Godfrey of the Agnes Irwin School, Susan M. Snyder of De Paul University, and consultant M. Suzann Duquette. Their insights and experiences as well as mine are reflected here.

Debbie Cohen deserves special thanks. From Debbie I learned how the process of writing proposals at a large institution differs from doing the same thing at a smaller one. We discovered that good proposals from large institutions such as MIT are quite similar to good proposals from smaller institutions such as Mount Holyoke and Lake Forest College, and that the differences have to do with scale, not content. Together we refined our ideas of what makes a successful proposal and why some ways of ordering and expressing ideas are more convincing than others. Debbie tackled the matter of format and developed the seven questions discussed in Chapter 2.

Thanks go, too, to Dick Johnson, research director at the Exxon Education Foundation, who suggested preparing costs and funding information in the manner described in Chapter 3, "The Budget." His counsel has been most welcome, and his sense of humor invaluable. Dick was our first special guest at the workshop, and I trust that his foreword gives my words as much credibility as his presence as "outside expert" did.

The workshop's popularity may reflect every new proposal writer's desire for guidance; it certainly reflects the ever-increasing importance of corporate and foundation support. Private institutions have been developing their relationships with corporations and foundations since the early 1970s, a process that accelerated towards the end of the decade. Labor-intensive, colleges and universities were neither able to pass on to students the full impact of rising prices for energy nor to cut deeply enough into operating costs, primarily personnel, to avoid raising fees. They economized where they could, deferring maintenance of facilities and holding down faculty salaries. Dramatic shifts in federal programs of student financial assistance beginning in 1981 intensified the need for additional funds.

Today most public and private colleges and universities, and many primary and secondary schools, are looking for corporate and foundation support. And increasingly such support, whether it takes the form of cash, equipment, personnel, or services, must be requested in writing. Someone at the hopeful institution prepares a document that asks for assistance, describes the desired form of this assistance and how it will be used, and backs up this request with persuasive reasons why the potential grantor should be interested in helping the institution. The proposal becomes part of a paper flood which threatens to submerge the desks of those foundation officers and corporate employees responsible for distributing a limited amount of money among many worthy causes.

The competition for corporate and foundation support is fierce, and the ability to write a proposal that will result in a grant is much in demand. Check the job listings—proposal writers are needed at schools and colleges, hospitals, museums, and social service organizations. The grants area is one of the fastest growing segments of the relatively new field of advancement, or development, and until very recently it was an area for which there was little formal training. Most of us in grants—indeed, most of us in fund raising—came in through the back door, so to speak. I don't know anyone who answered the question, "What do you want to do when you grow up?" with "I want to raise money." We were journalists, academics, bankers, volunteers, social workers, housewives, and administrators in a wide variety of organizations. And we found ourselves raising money, some of us on the telephone, some face to face, and some by writing proposals. We learned how to do it by doing it, by succeeding and by having our proposals turned down. We learned that the best way to cure writer's block (or stage fright) is to make yourself sit down and write (or stand up and write, if that's your preference) and that "doing your homework" is probably the most important factor in writing winning proposals.

The most important element in a proposal is acknowledgement of the "fit" between your institution's needs and the interests of the corporation or foundation that you are approaching. There's no such thing as the perfect proposal, or the perfect way to write a proposal, although all newcomers to the field would like to believe that such a template exists. Chapter 1, "Research," may explain why a proposal that raised thousands for my school won't do the same for yours if you simply change a few names. But you can learn a good deal from the experiences of those of us who've been in the business for a while, and this book draws heavily on the knowledge—and the wit, wisdom, and words—of some of the best proposal writers in the business.

One of the main points of this book is that in order to write successful proposals, you have to pay a great deal of attention to what the potential donor, corporation, or foundation wants to accomplish. You can't expect to get money just because your institution needs it; there's got to be some reward for the grantor, too. On the other hand, it is dangerous to orient yourself, or allow your institution to orient itself, too closely on the interests of the corporation or foundation. You should help your institution maintain its integrity. Don't let your faculty or administrators or your own mind be swayed by the trendy or the pragmatic. You may be correct in perceiving that corporations want to support business programs, for example, and that peace studies are bringing a lot of foundation dollars to college campuses. But that doesn't mean that you should encourage people at your college to adopt a business major or establish an institute for world peace. Don't distort the institution's mission just so you have a better chance to get grants.

I've dealt with quite a few people in education who are unrealistic in their understanding of "the grants business." The majority resemble in attitude the faculty members who were sure that corporations would support an endowed chair in Women's Studies "because they should feel guilty about the way they've treated women." But I have also talked with some who ask me what's being funded and say they'll dream up any sort of research as long as they can get a grant. Both attitudes are unproductive and ultimately self-defeating.

Fund raising is a new profession, and it's one that has an unfortunate record of abuses. Our part of fund raising comes in for its share of opprobrium. "Grantsmanship," it's called; the term implies a slickness and a willingness to perform all sorts of contortions to obtain money. To overcome this reputation, we must always act ethically, helping our institutions and the foundations and corporations we approach on their behalf to be open about their needs and goals. We must be honest about areas where interests don't overlap as well as where they do. We must say no as well as yes.

As we develop our skills and learn to know where compromise is possible and where it isn't, we must take great care that we are reflecting our institutions' policies, not trying to set them according to where we know funds are available. We exist to interpret, not to create, to serve the needs of our institutions, not to set their priorities. To do so well, we must maintain and share our institutions' visions, and we must sympathize with and work to achieve their goals by making those visions comprehensible to the individuals who control foundation and corporate resources. This is not an easy task. We won't be thanked by seeing our names in print, or by having buildings named after us, or even by receiving large paychecks. Knowing that our institutions are stronger because of our efforts must provide a substantial reward. We are the brokers, the bridges, the facilitators—and it's our insistence on the highest level of professionalism that will ensure that corporations, foundations, and educational institutions will continue to work together for the benefit of all.

Judith Mirick Gooch
Director of Development, School of Science
Massachusetts Institute of Technology

Chapter 1

Research

Submitting a proposal is only one step in the development of a relationship between your institution and an organization from which it is seeking support. While putting together the written document is crucial—you rarely get grants without asking for them—a lot of other things have to happen before you put that document in the mail if your institution is to have a chance of getting a favorable response. Good research is fundamental to writing successful proposals.

You're actually doing research all the time: talking with faculty and students, alumni, parents, friends; reading the daily newspaper as well as the "trade" papers and the monthly magazines; watching a TV special on volcanoes or flipping through the donor lists in the symphony program. You are absorbing massive amounts of information every moment of the day. What you learn to do, as a proposal writer, is to organize that information in certain ways.

Any grant you get is the result of how well your needs meet the *donor's* interests and needs. No matter how convincing your statistics, how strong your institution, how eloquent your prose, or how well your president knows the chair of the board, you're only going to get the grant if it's for a purpose that the donor finds appealing. Ron Coman of the Dart & Kraft Foundation says that corporate philanthropy is an oxymoron, and the same could be said of foundation philanthropy. Just as every contribution from an individual meets some need and provides some reward for the donor, every corporation or foundation grant will in some fashion advance the interests of the organization that makes it. Research is the process of identifying those areas of mutual interest, of figuring out where your institution's projects are likely to be most appealing, of learning what's in it for the donor. And this will be different for each foundation and corporation.

The need to focus on the donor's interest makes the shotgun method ineffective. Many people think that if you're sending out a lot of proposals, your chances of getting some financial return are better than if you're sending out only a few. That's true—but only if those proposals are aimed, rifle style, at the recipient. You can't treat corporate and foundation solicitation like a direct mail campaign. Word processing is wonderful, but it's dangerous, too. It's greatly increased the number of people who advocate taking a proposal prepared for Foundation A, changing the name and address, and sending it off to Corporation B (or to Corporations B through X, Y, and Z). After all, you don't have anything to lose, right?

Wrong. In the first place, your institution may waste an opportunity. A direct mail appeal to "cold" prospects—individuals with no previous tie to your institution or cause—may persuade 5 percent of its recipients to send contributions, but they won't be large ones. If you blanket the local corporations or mail your proposal to everyone in your state's foundation directory, you've used up your opportunity to approach these organizations. You've lost the chance to tailor an appeal that could result in a much larger grant and mark the beginning of a long and mutually profitable relationship.

Losing your credibility is another possible consequence of the shotgun approach. The philanthropic community has always been a small one—someone has estimated that there are perhaps 1,000 professional foundation positions in this country. And especially since the early 1980s, when federal policy began to shift responsibility for nonprofit funding out of the national pocket, the grant makers have banded together. The flood of proposals they receive leaves them little time to investigate each applicant. In self-defense, and in the consciousness of a growing professionalism, they've begun to ask each other for information. Your mass-mailed proposal will be seen for exactly what it is as soon as someone picks up the phone or the grant makers get together at the monthly meeting of the Donors' Circle or the 2% Club.

Word of mouth can be helpful if you enlist the representative from ABC Corporation, who knows your institution well and respects it, to persuade his or her opposite number at F & G Industries that the contributions committee should take a good look at your proposal. But you can't use that strategy with the shotgun method, which leaves all those potential donors with the impression that your institution doesn't know how to do things, that the development operation clearly isn't professional, and, by extension, the place probably isn't very well run. Given the competition for limited resources, and the intensity with which potential donors are examining the management of potential recipients, your chances of getting a grant from any of those corporations have just diminished substantially. Your institution will be served much better by fewer proposals, all of which clearly reflect the results of research.

Sometimes those in charge of your institution seem to encourage shotgun tactics. They like quantitative proof of activity. Even if you haven't gotten a lot of checks in the mail lately, being able to cite great numbers of proposals out there "working" strengthens your development report. But what do you do when the board inquires about the hit rate? Sending out proposals, no matter how many, isn't enough; they've got to generate grants.

I can't tell you how many times I've been asked for the "right" number of proposals to send out and what percentage should be getting funded. There is no answer to this except "It depends..." on your institution's size, mission, goals, priorities, needs, reputation, staff, and how well it uses its resources. And you are one of those resources, although your responsibilities at a large institution might differ tremendously from those of your colleagues who work at small colleges or preparatory schools.

If you work for a large institution with a well-developed fund-raising program, you might be handed the results of another staff member's research on the corporation or foundation for which you're going to write a proposal. In a small shop you're often expected to do it all. You identify a wide range of possible sources, screen the list for the most likely donors, choose the purpose and amount of the request, develop and orchestrate the strategy to prepare the organization to receive the proposal, and then write the proposal. But whether you do it all yourself or use materials someone else has prepared, you still have to go through the same steps in order to determine the shape and content of the proposal. To put together a convincing document you have to know the answers to these six questions:

- Who will read the proposal?
- What are the interests of the organization being addressed?
- What does the organization require in a proposal, in what form, and what are its deadlines?
- Why is your institution looking for funds—that is, what will the money enable you to do?
- What is involved in the activity being described, how long will it take, how much is it going to cost, what is it going to produce, and how are you going to measure your success?
- Why is there (or should there be) a relationship between the organization being approached and your institution?

A foundation or corporation always acts in its own interests, and it's up to you to find the areas where those interests overlap those of your institution. There are lots of sources of information. Your files, books and publications produced by independent firms, the organization's own annual reports and (sometimes) guidelines, newspapers, and magazines will get you started. You may have an alumnus (or several) employed at high levels in the corporation you want to approach. You, or someone in the development office, may call on the foundation's executive director or your president may visit the chair of the board.

Your counterparts at other institutions may be able to supply information, too. It's all right to ask for advice from someone at an institution that has gotten a grant from an organization you plan to approach. But do your homework first. I once had a call from a colleague asking how we got a Kresge Foundation grant. Before I launched into a description of the process, I inquired about the nature of her institution's building project. She replied that they were planning to ask for scholarships. Unfortunately, Kresge only supports bricks and mortar or major (million-dollar) pieces of equipment, a fact that is apparent from the most cursory scan of printed matter. A little research would have saved me some time and her considerable embarrassment.

The other gaffe to avoid is asking for a copy of another institution's proposal. People new to proposal writing (and sometimes presidents and faculty members) don't believe this, but seeing another institution's proposal won't help you. Your institution is unique, and therefore so is your project and your relationship with the potential donor. Someone else's words aren't going to describe those things that make your institution special and your proposal convincing. In today's competitive climate, you've got to make your institution visible. You can't do that by recirculating another institution's prose. You can get the information you need by talking with the person or people responsible for putting together the other institution's successful proposal.

Suppose you've just been handed an assignment to write a proposal to International Chemical Co. for $25,000 for need-based scholarships for chemistry majors. You need to know, at a minimum, how many chemistry students there are and how many are receiving financial assistance. You need basic information about how your institution determines financial need, the aid budget for an individual student, and what's being spent on aid for all students. Some historical perspective helps, too. Has the aid budget (or the number of chemistry majors) grown substantially? What's happening in the chemistry program that sounds unusual or exciting? Where are the majors going when they graduate? Are any of them working for International Chemical? Have they won prizes, invented marvelous new compounds, become teachers (and thus trainers of future chemistry majors)? Is the department enrolling a record number of pre-med students, all of whom are getting into medical school? Does the faculty have a particularly strong track record of getting grants? Does the department enroll unusual numbers of women or minorities? What sorts of facilities and equipment can you point to with pride?

The best source of that information is, of course, the faculty in the department. Perhaps your institution has a long tradition of expecting faculty to draft the major portion of a proposal and your part is to request a draft from the appropriate member of the department. Or perhaps you're expected to put the whole thing together from scratch. In either case, you'll become just as familiar with the data as the person giving you the information, for you're going to have to determine what should be included to convince the contributions committee at International Chemical and what should be omitted to avoid boring them. Your faculty experts will give you a tremendous amount of information. And right now, while you're doing research, you want it all. You can sort it out later.

Don't hesitate to go back, several times if necessary, for clarification. You're the one who has to make sure that technical matters are clear to the person with a limited technical background who reads the proposal, that statistics are not misleading, that sources are correctly cited. I've found that faculty are generally quite willing to explain things. They're in the business of making the unknown comprehensible, and in some ways you're just another student. Follow the same rule here: Make sure you've done your homework before yelling for help. Try to understand what they told you before you go back for explanations.

While you're learning about the chemistry program, you're also trying to find out more about International Chemical. The first place to look is in the files. Has your institution had grants from this company before? If so, for what? Has some-one been keeping in touch with the company about the ways in which that earli-er support helped (or continues to help) your faculty and students? Has the company had regular contact with your institution, receiving an annual report or a "summer letter" from the president or the department chair? Has someone called on the company president or the contributions officer recently? If so, what happened?

With many corporations, employment of alumni can be a vital factor in grant decisions. Which of your graduates are employed there? If the company is one of the more than 1,000 with a matching gifts program, you may be able to determine whether you have friends in high places (or at least a good placement record) by the number of matching gift transmittal letters or receipts. A word of caution here, though: It's probable that not all your alums who work at the company take ad-vantage of the matching gifts program, and it's also likely that some of those for whom you can find receipts have left the company. You'll need to check before dropping names. See whether your best contact at the company can obtain a list of your graduates employed there; many personnel offices maintain such lists, although they may be reluctant to share them. Sometimes your faculty can help. Many former students keep in touch with their favorite faculty through thick and thin, even though the alumni office hasn't heard from them since graduation.

Next, find out what the company has to say about itself. Read the corporate an-nual report. Pay attention to the company's financial health and what points it's trying to make in the pictures. Is it featuring environmental clean-up efforts or minority laboratory workers? Who's on the board and do you know any of them? If it has a foundation and publishes an annual report and guidelines for grant seek-ers, get them and read them. They're your best source. They'll tell you about dead-lines, format, fields of interest, and, equally important, what the organization will not fund. If the organization doesn't publish a report on its philanthropy (and unless a company has a foundation it is not required to do so), you'll have to begin with other publications, such as those listed in the bibliography at the end of this book.

Many foundations don't publish a report or guidelines, but all are required by the Internal Revenue Service to file annual financial statements. These PF 990s may be viewed at the Foundation Center in New York City or at any of the Foundation Center's cooperating collections across the country (see page 76). The PF 990 lists the foundation's income, assets and expenditures, grants paid by amount and recipient, and (usually) the foundation's officers, with their addresses. What it doesn't list are fields of interest or restrictions, but you can generally deduce a good deal by looking at the grants. If all the recipients are Catholic hospitals, you can assume that the foundation is unlikely to be interested in your community col-lege. If the largest grant is $2,500, your request for $45,000 is probably out of line. If all the grants in recent years have gone to organizations in Nebraska and Flori-da, you can probably assume that your prep school in Maine doesn't stand a chance. Occasionally you'll discover an unusual circumstance that allows you to break the rules; if the foundation's president is an alumnus of your school, you should en-courage someone to talk with him or her. There may well be some possibilities for support that aren't immediately obvious.

Direct contact between someone from your institution and a representative of the corporation or foundation is one of the most productive methods of research. Whether you are calling on a program officer at a major foundation or a community relations representative at a corporation, or whether your president and the chair of the board are calling on the president and chair of the corporation or foundation, the information collected will be straight from the horse's mouth. What are the board's latest concerns? How is the money holding out? Is the program officer seeing a lot more proposals for computer equipment, and has this led to any changes in policy? A visit allows the caller to convey news about your institution. This might not be directly related to the proposal topic but it could set the stage for a successful reception by persuading the organizational representative that your institution is in great shape. You can often try out the ideas you plan to express in the proposal, and the reaction from the corporation or foundation person may have a marked effect on the shape of the final draft.

The final stage of research is putting together all the data you've assembled, whether you get it in a report from the research staff and a draft from the chair of the chemistry department or whether you've gathered it all. Take a hard look at what you've got. Do you understand enough about how the new piece of equipment works to be able to explain it in writing to someone without a chemistry background? Can you cite an impressive number of graduates employed at International Chemical, or should you begin to think of an appendix that lists all the competing companies employing your alumni? Do you need projections for next year's financial aid expenditures? Should the president schedule a visit with the president of the foundation now, well in advance of the proposal deadline? And are you allowing enough time to prepare the proposal, get it looked at by everyone who needs to approve it, and still get it delivered on time? If so, you're ready for the next stage of proposal writing: organizing your material.

Chapter 2

Organizing Your Material

You've collected vast amounts of information about the project or purpose for which you're going to request funds, and you know quite a lot about the corporation or foundation to which the proposal will be sent. How do you sort out what you know, determine what you still need to find out, choose what's most appropriate to use, and put it in a convincing order?

Every proposal, whether it consists of two pages or 25, whether it's requesting $1,000 or $100,000, and whether the need being described is simple or complex, has to provide the person who reads it with enough information to make a decision. You'd like to make sure that the decision is positive, and therefore you need to provide persuasive answers to the questions a potential grant maker is most likely to ask. These are:

1. What's the problem?
2. What's the solution?
3. How are you going to solve the problem?
4. Why is your institution qualified to do it?
5. What do you need (time, money, people) to do it?
6. How will you measure your success?
7. Why should this particular corporation or foundation fund this particular project at your institution?

Defining the problem

Imagine that you are a member of International Chemical's contributions committee. Every month or six weeks you're asked to look over almost 200 requests for funds, and you do this in addition to carrying out the other responsibilities of your senior position. What do you see over and over again? "Give us money be-

7

cause we need it... for our youth hostel, for our museum, to balance our budget, to buy books. We have a problem, you have a solution—money."

How much more appealing is an opening that describes a situation affecting International Chemical and proposes a way to change the situation for the better. "Recognizing the national shortage of trained chemists, Ivy College has designed a program that will enable chemistry majors to complete the full chemistry curriculum in three rather than four years." That opening speaks to every member of the contributions committee and convinces them all that they should keep reading: Ivy College may be able to do something for International.

Defining the problem so that it will interest the organization receiving the request is the most critical aspect of writing a successful proposal, and it's one of the most difficult tasks. The people on the inside—your colleagues on campus, up to and including the president—are caught up in the day-to-day needs of your institution. They naturally fall into the habit of institution-centered thinking. The president looks at projections for faculty salaries and thinks, "We really need more endowed chairs," while the person responsible for the physical plant sees the need for a new boiler or tuckpointing Old Boy Hall. When you're asked to write a request for a grant to fund these things, there's a tendency to assume that the need is justified merely because it exists. And so it may seem to those at the institution. But your need alone is never enough to get a grant. You have to meet one or more of the donor's needs, too.

The results of your research should help you define your institution's need in terms of a problem of concern to the potential donor. A very wise person once said that in the grants business, as in individual giving, you should never forget that people give to people. The institutions—yours and the one you're planning to approach—are simply the vehicles for passing on the benefits. And problems can almost invariably be defined in relation to people. Remembering that may help you focus on the way that a new instrument will help students learn to become chemists (and thus produce a steady stream of well-trained potential employees for International) rather than on how much the department "needs" state-of-the-art equipment. An endowed chair is important not because the endowment income helps balance the operating budget, although it does this, but because the chair's incumbent is enabled to teach more students, or to teach more effectively, or to pursue additional research, or in some other fashion to prepare students to succeed.

Why should a foundation or corporation pay for your new boiler? Because adequate facilities enable faculty to do a better job of teaching and students of learning, thus adding to the world's supply of well-educated people. What about a grant to improve library services—how does that meet donor needs? Students and faculty need access to as much data as possible so that they can learn and teach most effectively. A library provides access.

What about that hardest sell of all, unrestricted operating support? Admittedly, this case is ever harder to make, but let's go back to people helping people. The students at your institution are going to be consumers, community members, voters, employees, parents, taxpayers. They may be the leaders of business and industry, the doctors, the lawyers, the college professors who will mold the minds of the next generations. Isn't it important to us all to have them as well-prepared as possible for their roles? And isn't your institution a great place to prepare them, for reasons you'll enumerate to the potential grantor?

Defining a problem to suit corporate needs can be easy, if your graduates work for the company or your faculty consult on special projects. The company has a vested interest in helping your institution continue to do well what it's already doing or to explore related areas. But self-interest doesn't rest solely in the recruiting relationship. Corporations employ lots of people, many of whom live in the community in which the corporation is based. The corporation is therefore interested in making sure that the community is a good place to live because if it isn't, the corporation may have trouble hiring and keeping its workers. The argument that a program meets a community need, thereby improving the quality of life, is especially potent for social service groups, but educational institutions shouldn't neglect it either. Maybe your secondary school enrolls children of middle management personnel or your community college offers exciting programs for their elderly parents. Employees may use your sports facilities, attend your film or art festivals, and take continuing education courses unrelated to their careers but refreshing to their intellects.

Match the scope of your institution's need or idea to the size of the corporation. In the case of International Chemical Co., a multinational organization, show that you recognize the magnitude of the problem. Define it as a worldwide—or at least a national—shortage of trained chemists, especially if you can point to an international or at least a national student body. If, on the other hand, you are approaching a purely local organization, or your institution serves primarily those who come from the local area and tend to remain there, you'll want to define the need in terms of a local shortage of well-trained personnel.

Foundation giving is usually a little more altruistic. Foundations must pay out a certain portion of their income in the form of grants, so you don't have to convince them that grant making is a good thing to do. But you still have to identify your institution's need in terms of the foundation's interests, which usually refer to the original donor's wishes. Perhaps the founder wanted to increase the number of people becoming research chemists. Other foundations have been established to solve other problems: to fund a search for cancer cures, encourage the study of foreign languages, or develop closer relationships between Canada and the United States. As I mentioned in Chapter 1, it's crucial to pay attention to the foundation's definition of its interests, because even with the best wishes or intentions a foundation executive can't make a grant if the purpose isn't allowed under the rules. Corporations have the potential for much more flexibility, although their lack of legal constraint is balanced by the need to respect the interests of management, representing their shareholders. In practice, most restrict themselves to a narrow range of problems.

Many local foundations are interested in improving the quality of life. As with corporations, you'll need to identify a local need—such as inadequate recreation facilities for teenagers—and to strengthen your request for funds for a sports center by pointing out that your new swimming pool will be open to the public during certain hours. Quality of life can appeal to a major national foundation, as well, if you have developed a program of special education for the elderly, for instance, that could be copied by community colleges across the country.

The scope of your problem plays a role in foundation solicitation, too. A major regional or national foundation is going to be interested in a project that meets a need (solves a problem) of similar scope. The Fords, Carnegies, and Mellons won't help you build a dormitory, but they might be very interested in a radical new plan to encourage early retirement of senior faculty by helping them train for second careers. This sort of project would be meeting a need experienced by nearly every academic institution in the country, and if your institution appears capable of managing the experiment, the bigger foundations might well help you try it.

If you're having trouble writing a proposal, reexamine your definition of the problem. It should be focused on the interests of the corporation or foundation, because it's the cornerstone of your entire document and determines the shape of all that follows.

Identifying the solution

Once you've decided what the problem is from the potential grant maker's point of view, you can proceed to the much easier step of describing the solution. Here, too, it's crucial to focus on the grantor. You've probably known the solution all along, usually well before you could articulate the problem. Be careful, though. Circumstances and institution-centered thinking can easily lead you into a false identification of the solution.

What often happens is that the chair of the chemistry department tells you about the new scanning electron microscope the department wants to purchase. "Our students need better cell biology courses. The problem is that we don't have a scanning electron microscope." When you focus on the interest of the potential grant maker, you perceive that the *real* problem is a lack of cell biologists, and the solution is better training, including experience on advanced instrumentation. Lack of an electron microscope is the institution's problem, not the donor's. Just as the problem must be defined in terms broad enough to encompass corporate or foundation interests, the solution, too, must be related to the concerns of the corporation or foundation.

Take the case of an endowed chair in chemistry. A chair is a solution for your institution's problem. For the potential grantor the solution is better teaching and the problem is poorly trained employees. The chair is the means by which the institution and the grantor will solve the problem, but in itself it is not the solution. If providing a suitable education for bright young people is the problem, helping talented but needy students attend your institution is a solution, and scholarships are one way of achieving that goal.

Define the solution *briefly*. Think of it as one of those 25-words-or-less contests. If you're finding it difficult to boil down the solution to a phrase, you're probably not seeing the problem clearly. The definition of the solution should be a mirror image of your definition of the problem. The country's symphony orchestras need more violinists? We will train them. Seventeen percent of the inner-city residents are unemployable because of illiteracy? We will teach them to read.

How you're going to reach—and teach—those illiterate adults, find more children with musical talent and provide training, or develop a cure for cancer, you'll deal with later. For now, limit yourself to saying that you're going to do it.

How to do it

This part of proposal development is often the easiest. Usually it's where you started; the people involved with the project or concerned about the need (as it's perceived on campus) came to you with ideas, plans, details, and excitement. Your main problem may be to sort the important from the extraneous. It's rarely difficult to get enough information about what someone wants to do, although as you begin to write you will almost always find some holes to fill.

In the beginning of this chapter, I quoted the opening of a proposal from (fictitious) Ivy College. "Recognizing the national shortage of trained chemists, Ivy College has designed a program that will enable chemistry majors to complete the full chemistry curriculum in three rather than four years." The problem is stated; a solution—training chemists faster—is easily inferred. Now you can think about how you're going to enable those students to complete in three years a rigorous curriculum which at every other institution takes four. This is where you begin to tackle the nuts and bolts of the plan. Does the department intend to offer summer sessions? Redesign certain courses? Add computer-based self-teaching modules which students can use on weekends?

Now's the time to consider why this particular method of solving the problem is the most effective. Make the department chair explain so that you can understand (and convey the explanation to the potential funder) why cramming more classroom and laboratory time into the same calendar will help students learn more, faster, or why adopting a summer semester for chemistry majors is a more effective pedagogical device than adding more material to the standard curriculum. Have other institutions tried this? Is your faculty aware of similar efforts and why they succeeded or failed?

If you're looking for endowment for faculty salaries (and remember that the need, as expressed to the donor, is for better teaching), here's where you cluster ideas about the merits of a chair as the vehicle for encouraging better teaching. Why a chair—why not just more money for merit pay or for across-the-board salary increases? What is there about a chair that makes it a desirable means of rewarding good teaching or inspiring improvements? You know some of the answers: recognition; additional support and prestige for the incumbent; encouragement to the discipline or department; incentives for junior faculty; reknown for the individual, the department, and the institution; and so on. The "whys" will vary depending on your definition of the problem, which depends on the potential grantor's interests.

Suppose you're approaching a family foundation for an endowed chair in music (this is how you're going to solve the problem of too few violinists). You know that the man who established the foundation was a frustrated violinist. So you justify "how" you will solve the problem by stressing that a chair will call attention to the importance of outstanding teaching of violin. It will have substantially more impact than merely funding another teaching position.

If your institution's goal is more endowed scholarships for violin students, you might point out that the possibility of being a named scholar will attract the most talented young people to your music program. "What" you want to do is educate more talented students, thus filling a need for (solving the problem of) too few violinists; "how" is to provide scholarships; and "why" is the prestige of the award as well as the availability of the funds.

Making the case for a project or program is far easier than making the case for unrestricted support. A project gives you lots of concrete details to discuss, and the only danger is losing sight of the concept behind the plan. Operating support is much more difficult to justify, but it can be done. If you have correctly identified the problem as a need for the kinds of services that your institution provides, you can now identify specific examples of those services. Often, you're approaching a local corporation or foundation for such unrestricted support, so your examples would usually revolve around the way in which your institution improves the quality of life in the community.

What you need to do it

You've described your plan of action—what you're going to do to solve the problem. Now you need to get down to the basic details: What will it take to do what you plan to do? What do you need—time, people, equipment, space—to carry out your plan? And why these particular resources?

Demonstrating a thorough understanding of what resources you need is a good way of convincing a potential donor to become an actual contributor, because it shows that you have thought through your plan. Obviously, some plans require more types of support than others. For an endowed chair or scholarships, what you need is money. Stating the amount required to endow a chair is not the same as putting in a budget (we'll get to budgets later), but you'll need to explain why your institution sets the price of a chair at $500,000 or $1,500,000. Why require a minimum of $50,000 to endow a scholarship? Perhaps because the college uses only 6 percent of the income from an endowed fund and the average grant award from institutional resources is $3,000. Don't just take it for granted that the amount justifies itself, or that "everyone" funds endowments at this level. Ask the experts, the ones who decided on the amount.

When the proposal deals with a project such as curriculum development, the amount of detail can appear endless. Later, when you are editing the proposal, you may want to eliminate some of those details from the written document (although you shouldn't forget to allow for them in the budget). Right now you need to work closely with the people involved in the project to identify every item they even suspect they might need.

Let's say you are going to request a grant to revise the foreign language curriculum. Members of the language department have decided that they need to develop courses in French, Spanish, and Japanese for business majors, and that all introductory courses ought to be offered intensively. They must also gear up for the new institution-wide foreign language requirement, and they want to offer a special major in Romance languages. What will they need to implement these plans?

The easiest need to identify is almost always personnel. In this case, the department wants another full-time faculty member in Japanese, and released time so faculty members can develop the business/language courses. (This means your institution may hire a replacement faculty member to teach the course from which the regular faculty member is released.) To strengthen the introductory courses in which the majority of students will enroll to fulfill the language requirement, the department wants to offer special language training via computer; no one has found any appropriate software on the market, so someone will be needed to write the programs. This could be an outside consultant or—if you have the capability—an in-house expert. You will probably find that only the major needs—the full-time appointment in Japanese, for example—will surface in your initial conversations with the project people. The rest will come to light during the development of the budget.

What they're planning will require some equipment: a microcomputer with Japanese characters, a special printer, floppy disks, etc. The micro will be used by students later when the Japanese business course is implemented, and in fact another one will also be needed at that time. The expected increase in the number of students taking language courses will require additional stations in the language laboratories and more tapes and cassettes.

Developing a major in Romance languages won't require much more than identifying a sequence of courses. But the department wants to call attention to the program by bringing in a series of guest lecturers and arranging opportunities for students to work with various foreign scholars. This requires some coordination, which can be provided by the member of the faculty appointed to chair the major.

What's the timetable? How soon is your institution going to start graduating students able to communicate with foreign business people in their native languages? When will it be sending students to graduate programs in Romance languages? You'll probably have to help the project people figure that out, and you may find yourself getting into the workings of the academic community in ways you never dreamed. The language faculty will have to shepherd course changes through the faculty committees that must approve them, but you often need to make sure that they've allowed the necessary time to do this. It can take more than a year before a new course can be taught, since it must be approved and then published in the catalog before students can enroll. Signing up famous speakers can take time, too.

Keeping track of the timing can be especially tricky if you are dealing with a large project involving a lot of people and covering a span of several years. You may want to have something on paper for your own use and for those involved in the project. Depending on the requirements of the potential funder and the complexity of the activities, you may want to include this timetable with the proposal. Flow charts with all sorts of arrows and boxes were quite popular a few years ago. Some people swear by time-line graphs. Whatever method you choose to keep track of who is supposed to do what at what time, make sure that it's comprehensible to those whom it is intended to help.

Why us?

You've already spent a good deal of time thinking about why your project would be interesting to a particular foundation or corporation, and you've defined your need in a manner that reflects your understanding of those interests. Now you need to pay attention to the reasons why your institution is uniquely qualified to solve the problem you've defined. What can you point to that will convince a corporate or foundation board not only that you've hit on a problem that needs to be solved and designed an appropriate solution, but that your institution is capable of implementing that solution?

One thing that might influence a potential donor would be your institution's record in the area you're addressing. Does your institution already graduate a lot of language majors, good violinists, or chemists? Can you prove it by the numbers of your alumni employed as chemists by the company you're approaching, or the numbers of first violins who were trained by your faculty? If you need more space for the business program, can you point to middle managers for whom the business school has set up special training courses? In short, will this grant build on past success?

If you're looking for funds that will help your institution explore a new area or an area new to your institution, you'll have to rely on less direct evidence of capability. In preparing a proposal that describes efforts with a special segment of your students, perhaps you can cite another teaching project that your institution has carried out. Or you may have to strengthen your case for support of revising the foreign language programs by giving some brief examples of successful projects.

Describe the qualifications of the people who will be guiding the project. Their past success lends credibility to your claim. Point to the qualifications of your students, if possible. Why are they uniquely suited to benefit from the efforts being undertaken on their behalf? Are they particularly capable—or greatly in need of help that only your institution can provide? Do you have special facilities, such as a foundry, that will enable students enrolled in the new studio sculpture course to cast their pieces? Will your location in the heart of the city help you attract continuing education students at lunchtime and in the early evening?

Signs that your institution thinks this project or purpose is important will strengthen your case. Institutions that agree to devote substantial resources (people, space, time, money) to the cause are demonstrating commitment in a tangible way. But money isn't the only proof of commitment. What percent of your faculty or student body will be affected by what you plan to do, and will they be active participants or passive recipients? A project that will revitalize the teaching faculty is much more impressive if at least half your faculty members have agreed to participate in the series of workshops. The new foreign language requirement involved in the curriculum revision makes that entire project appealing. Not only will it lead to better educated students, which is the primary goal, but every undergraduate will be involved.

"Why us?" can also be bolstered by a general aura of competence. An institution that has been able to balance its budgets is much more attractive to an organization that might "invest" in it than one with a record of deficit spending. And you should cite recent grants from other foundations and corporations, especially if they were made for purposes similar to the one for which you are now seeking support.

Foundation and corporation boards like to stick together; they often feel safer giving to institutions that have already received grants from significant givers. This is tough if your institution hasn't been in the grants business for long or hasn't had any major success. We all envy the Harvards and Stanfords when we look at their donor lists, which appear to include every Fortune 500 company and the equivalent in the foundation world. But it's always possible to "get on the list," and that first big grant, or small grant from a key corporation or foundation, can have an impact all out of proportion to its dollar amount. That, too, can be a reason to cite as you develop the case for your institution, as we'll see later.

Evaluation

How are you going to measure the success of your project? How are you going to show your grantor that the corporate or foundation funds were well spent? Your proposal has to convince the grant maker that your institution is responsible. One of the ways to prove this is to describe how you're going to demonstrate that you've succeeded, that you've done what you said you were going to do.

For those who've been involved in government-funded projects, the word "evaluation" may conjure up specters of forms, masses of papers filed in 10 copies with extra cover pages, and requests for additional information. All, of course, ask for information in a form different from the way your institution maintains it. (That's part of Murphy's Law as it applies to grant seekers.) But evaluations don't have to be complicated. Keep in mind that the donor wants to know that the organization's money has helped achieve the results for which it was intended, and that the recipient institution has fulfilled its share of the bargain.

An evaluation consists of three parts: a discussion of what worked, what didn't, and why; a detailed accounting of expenditures, including ways in which the money was actually spent that differed from those described in the request, and why; and a description of what will happen next. Your proposal, therefore, needs to contain as part of its plan some references to your expectations. You've already outlined the expected results in your description of the solution to the problem you're addressing; here, you can add more detail. Do you intend to increase enrollments in foreign language programs by 25 percent? Graduate 15 students each year who go to work for multinational corporations? Quantifiable data is always helpful, and you should ask those proposing a project to identify areas in which some measurements are possible. This will greatly strengthen your proposal.

If you're asking for bricks-and-mortar money, you'll evaluate the project by whether the building is completed on time and within budget, and whether it serves the population for which it was intended in the ways planned. You'll also be concerned with the efficiency of its operation and perhaps even with its architectural impact. Are you doing anything unusual to raise the money, such as challenging alumni or parents? If so, an evaluation will measure the success of the fund-raising effort. A bricks-and-mortar proposal won't dwell on evaluation as a project proposal will, but it will certainly refer to the budget, timetable, and planned use of the structure. Thinking ahead to telling the corporation or foundation how its money was spent can help you make sure your plan is complete.

Use some caution in setting up the scales on which you want your success to be measured. Just like grade inflation, too-high expectations of performance can destroy your institution's credibility. The proposers of a project are naturally inclined to think that their efforts will cure cancer and ensure world peace in six month's time, and this enthusiasm is necessary and welcome—it will carry them through the process of developing the project and writing the proposal. But you need to keep that enthusiasm within bounds when it comes to predicting success. Is it really likely that the purchase of a Microvax II will make every student computer literate? (And how are you going to measure computer literacy?) Will that endowment for sabbatical support really inspire every member of the music department to undertake a research project? It's a lot more impressive to tell a donor that the grant enabled you to exceed your goal, that you've graduated 105 chemists in the past three years instead of the 92 that you predicted, that minority enrollment is up to 12 percent rather than the 10.5 percent expected.

Don't set your sights too low either. You're trying to convince the potential donor that a grant will make a difference, that you'll accomplish something you couldn't do without it. Be positive. And be honest. Research frequently leads into paths entirely different from those anticipated; you can't possibly predict what that famous physicist will discover when the grant lets her lock herself in the laboratory with the new optics equipment. Your proposal rides on her reputation, and it's her accomplishments that will persuade the donor to invest in her research. You can surely expect results, but talk about general areas of exploration. When you report to the donor, you'll be able to point to some positive outcomes, even if they were unintended. If you've set too many standards in advance, the negatives may outweigh the positives. Leave room for flexibility.

You won't want to describe in detail the steps you'll take after the grant is expended. In some instances it's not necessary; a grant for endowment, for instance, won't be expended. But you may want to describe in the proposal the procedures by which a chair's incumbent will be appointed, the length of time someone may hold a chair, and any special tasks expected of the named individual. By doing this you set the stage for a report to the grantor: "Professor Jones was appointed by the faculty committee, with the approval of the Provost, for a term of five years. He has already begun to organize the senior seminar in Provençal poetry required of all students enrolled in the new Romance languages major."

"What next?" is very important to some grantors, and when you're dealing with a project, it can be extremely complex. Ask the proposers to think ahead to the end of the project and tell you what they'll want to do next. Do they plan to share the results with other people on campus or with other institutions? Do they plan to present findings at professional meetings or to publish them? If all goes as planned, will the institution or department modify its programs in some permanent fashion or otherwise make use of all this effort?

Often, when you ask the proposers what next, they'll respond that they want to continue the activity. So you have to plan for future funding, and mentioning this is one of the key indications to a potential donor that you've been thinking ahead: "After your money is gone, we intend to seek funding from..." or "...the institution will assume the costs of continuing the project." That's music to the ears of a potential donor. Just like a good budget, it indicates foresight; it demonstrates the institution's commitment to the idea. And if the institution isn't committed, there's no reason for anyone else to get involved.

Special reasons

Related to "why us?" though different in subtle but critical ways, is the final matter to be considered: Why are you sending this particular proposal to this particular foundation or corporation?

As you've developed the answers to the questions we considered above, you've been refining your argument continually, going from the widest possible focus to the most specific reasons why your institution qualifies for consideration. Now's your chance to note any other areas of mutual interest. Has the foundation or corporation made other grants to your institution (and is therefore in a good position to judge your competence)? Is its chair a member of your board of trustees? (Play this particular card with care and only with the consent of the person involved.) If the corporation is next door to your institution, talk about good neighbors. If employees' children (or employees themselves) study music with your faculty or use your swimming pool, you'll want to mention that, even if your proposal concerns computer equipment.

Here's where you can point, very subtly, to less direct benefits to the foundation or corporation, such as publicity (or lack of it) and the good company the donor would be keeping if it joined the list of contributors to your institution. Identify the less direct but equally important benefits to your institution: the leverage a grant would give you (that's a compliment to the donor) and the effect it could have on morale or on the operating budget.

Seats on the 50-yard line, however, are not appropriate special reasons, nor can you offer a corporation a certain number of graduates or open access to faculty research. You are asking for a grant, not selling a product or service, despite the way we talk about marketing our institutions. You might want to offer to name a building or a scholarship, but be sure you're not promising more than your institution will want to (or is allowed to) deliver. Organizations or individuals giving

17

scholarships to your institution are not legally permitted to select the beneficiaries, and naming privileges often carry a hefty price tag, such as a minimum of 50 percent of the cost of the building. What's the policy at your institution? Make sure you know it, and consider with care whether the potential donor is likely to be swayed or offended by the mention of such an incentive. Some want minimal public recognition, and with those wanting more, you can always discuss the means after you've gotten the grant. Some organizations specify the recognition they consider appropriate; recipients of certain grants are known as Watson Fellows, for example, after the founder of IBM. But generally, you shouldn't talk about recognition in a proposal unless you're putting in writing something that has already been discussed with foundation or corporate personnel.

The desire to perpetuate the memory of the company's founder may require some activities on the part of the institution receiving a corporate grant, but it will usually send some contributions your way in the first place only when the founder had a strong connection with your institution. It's the rare corporation that will provide funds enough to name a building or endow a chair—and the rare institution that will receive them. These days a company might pick up part of the tab for facilities in which its current or future employees are trained, but many companies prefer to support people and programs rather than bricks and mortar.

A foundation is more likely than a corporation to be interested in perpetuating the memory of an individual. After all, foundations are established to perpetuate the wishes, and thus the influence, of one or more people. But you can't assume that your need for a new art building will appeal to the Richard Nouveau Family Foundation just because you'll call it the Noveau Art Institute. Old Mr. Nouveau made his money in railroads and directed that his fortune be used to perpetuate free enterprise. If you could define a need for students to learn about entrepreneurship via the Richard Nouveau Endowed Professorship, you'd be in better shape.

Many people are surprised to learn that the institution's need to earn a challenge grant is rarely a special incentive for a corporation or foundation. Generally, challenges stimulate contributions from individuals; they build excitement and a sense of competition among your various constituencies. They give people a good reason to respond to an emotional appeal. But to a corporate or foundation board, the importance of your challenge grant lies in the fact that another organization—or individual—thinks well enough of your institution to make a sizeable financial commitment to it. Unless it's a family foundation with close ties between its board members and your institution, an organization won't be persuaded to contribute by your need to qualify for a challenge grant.

However, requesting a corporate or foundation grant to be used to challenge people to contribute can be very persuasive indeed. You'll need to show that the cause is appealing to your potential individual donors, and that they have the capacity to come up with the required amount. You'll need a well-designed plan for the fund-raising activities. In fact, you'll really prepare a proposal in miniature and slip it into the request. It's an extra effort, but sometimes well worth it because the foundation or corporation can see clearly that it's not paying the whole bill.

Is a capital campaign a special reason for a grant? Sometimes. A few foundations and corporations will give only to needs within the context of a campaign; others will never support them. When in doubt, ask. Never assume that because the president, the board, and the entire development staff are wildly excited about—or heavily involved in—a capital campaign, a potential grant maker will care about it. A grant may help you meet the goal, but that's your concern, not necessarily something that interests the corporation or foundation. Describing your campaign may reassure potential grantors about your institution's fiscal health and good management, but except in unusual circumstances, it won't guarantee a grant. And despite the announcements you can sometimes see, foundations and corporations rarely make grants "to the capital campaign." That money was awarded for specific purposes included among the campaign goals—for equipment or salaries or bricks and mortar.

Corporate support can generate good publicity for the corporation. On your campus, students can learn computing on DEC and IBM equipment and perhaps develop brand loyalty and an openness to recruitment. Faculty, too, can develop a commitment to certain vendors that could be important when someone engaged in research needs to purchase equipment or services. Off campus, publicity as a corporate "good guy" can help counteract a negative image. The oil companies are a case in point. When the price of gasoline, and thus corporate profits, started to go through the roof, corporate contributions for very visible good causes and cultural events increased substantially. IBM talks about its support of specific colleges and universities in full-page ads, getting credit for philanthropy and incidentally providing good publicity for the named institutions.

Publicity is not usually a factor in foundation decisions. Unlike corporations, foundations have nothing to sell. In fact some foundations won't allow their names to appear on plaques or donor lists because foundation personnel are inundated with requests every time news of a grant is published. (Of course these foundations must still file their grants lists with the IRS.)

Mentioning tax deductibility of grants will not strengthen your case. The tax break is not an incentive for foundations and not a very powerful one for corporations, especially in light of the recent changes. A grant may not "cost" as much as its face value because it can be deducted before taxes, but it still represents money that could have been paid out as salary or as shareholder dividends; profits invested in plant or equipment are deductible, too.

Perhaps conversations between your president and the foundation's executive director have preceded submission of the proposal—and you certainly hope there's been some direct contact between your institution and the organization. A particularly good "special" reason to send the proposal would be that the director (or chair of the board) suggested you do so. But exercise caution in using personal contacts. Your request should stand on its own merits; you can't count on friendship to bolster a weak idea. One misplaced appeal to the old boy network or the old school tie, or one effort to use clout to put across an inferior proposal can condemn your institution to years of refusals from that organization.

Keep track of reasons you mention in various other sections of your proposal. Some may be strong enough to reiterate. Do you train the corporation's employees?

Has the foundation often supported you? Look for other ways of setting your institution apart from the rest. Do you have an excellent reputation for handling your finances? (At least one college has made almost $100 million with investments of venture capital.) Do you number among your faculty or alumni body Nobel prize-winners, Olympic champion swimmers, or an unusual concentration of American Indians? Is your campus noted for its designer buildings or its status as a national aboretum?

Pick and choose and make sure that the "particularity" you cite has some relevance to your project, but don't assume that the reader will make the connection; you need to spell it out. The person to whom the proposal is addressed may be able to read between the lines, but you may need to educate the other people who will read it. Even if the recipient is going to summarize your proposal without sharing the document that conveys it, remember that your request is one of many. Make it easy for the reader; tell the whole story.

Chapter 3

The Budget

The budget is a critical part of every proposal. It explains in detail the amount you're requesting from the foundation or corporation. All the words in the proposal are the frosting on the cake; they're supposed to make the numbers in the budget taste good.

A budget is a plan, and building a budget is a superb planning exercise. It enables you and those involved with the project to clarify and specify the precise activities that they want to undertake. The process of clarification often provides information that helps them design a better project and helps you write a better proposal. Building a budget forces people to pin down their ideas. You will often find, for example, that those involved in the project may have decided they need "about $100,000" but they can't tell you exactly what they need it for, other than some vague generalities about summer salary and secretarial support. Your role is to help them figure out how long the project will take, how much it will really cost, and how much is really needed. You often get to do the arithmetic. One caution: Many faculty members seem to be terrified of budgets. If you are good at putting a budget together, you run the risk of being regarded as a miracle worker. If the project is funded, you may find that the faculty regard you as the money person and prefer to deal with you, rather than the business office, in the matter of expenditures.

A useful budget must be honest, accurate, and appropriately detailed. It must reflect the true costs of meeting the needs you're describing in the proposal. If your proposal is funded, the budget becomes the working document on which your institution bases its activities and the foundation or corporation bases its payments, and your institution will have to account for the expenditure of those funds. In one sense, the budget becomes a legal document; in the absence of any other formal statement, it's your contract with the granting organization. Your auditors certainly look at budgets of funded proposals and compare them to expenditures of record, and your institution is responsible to the foundation or corporate donor in the matter of expenditures.

To build a budget you need to know what's being done, who's going to do it, and how long it will take. You need a calculator with working batteries (or, better yet, an adding machine) and a good understanding of basic arithmetic, including how to find percentages. You need to know whom to ask about specific costs. And you need confidence in your ability. Take it from someone who suffers from severe math anxiety: It's not hard to prepare a budget. It can be tedious, but it can also be relaxing. It's not as amorphous as writing; you're dealing with numbers, which either add up or don't.

There are three questions you have to answer to design the budget to accompany any proposal:
- What will the project cost?
- How will the costs be covered?
- How much are you requesting from the particular organization to which this proposal is being sent?

Establishing the cost of the *entire* project is extremely important, regardless of the amount you plan to request from the foundation or corporation. No one, from the president on down, likes to discover halfway through a project that the institution is facing an unanticipated major cost that must be covered in order to finish the project. So part of your task is to figure out every conceivable activity connected with the project or purpose for which you're requesting funds, and attach a dollar figure to it. Using that information, you and those involved in the program can make some determination about which costs the institution might plan to cover and which might be requested from outside sources.

The following case study describes a new program that will cost a great deal to implement. For a project of this magnitude you could well be approaching a variety of corporations and foundations for support.

Case study: International Ventures Program

You are the proposal writer for the University of River City, located in Mainstream, Ohio, a city with close to 100,000 residents, which is trying to move its industrial base from steel-related manufacturing to high tech. URC enrolls 2,400 undergraduate men and women in its schools of arts and sciences, engineering, and business. About two-thirds of the undergraduates are full-time students, and most live on campus. URC also attracts a substantial number of local, part-time students to programs in the division of continuing education, although the number has diminished in recent years. A graduate program in business draws many of its students from the middle management ranks at local corporations.

The university has decided to strengthen the international emphasis of its curriculum throughout the disciplines and schools. It is felt that this will increase undergraduate enrollments, attracting students interested in careers in international business, working for multinational concerns, or joining the State Department. Local residents who work for the high-tech firms may be interested in certain business courses, and the community in general will be served by an expanded program of cultural activities. The new thrust may also appeal to corporations with programs of support for higher education, especially Worldwide Computer, Inc., which has recently opened a major manufacturing facility in Mainstream.

The curriculum revision committee, an ad hoc group that includes faculty from all divisions and disciplines, administrators, students, and trustees, has recommended certain changes. These include reinstituting a foreign language requirement in the School of Arts and Sciences; requiring all undergraduates to take at least one course that deals with another culture; developing an overseas internship program; adding courses in the economics of developing countries and Japanese management style to the business curriculum; expanding an existing executive-on-campus program to include representatives from foreign companies; opening the foreign film series to the public; and adding two major displays of art from other cultures to the university gallery's yearly schedule of exhibitions.

The new language requirement will mean adding three full-time positions in the foreign language department, more stations to the language laboratory, and new tapes, books, and periodicals to the library. Advanced students will be trained to act as peer tutors. The School of Arts and Sciences already offers a substantial number of courses dealing with other cultures, but URC will need to add a part-time position in history to be certain that there will be enough sections to handle the demand for the Far Eastern Culture course.

The placement office will need to add a half-time position to develop the overseas internships; it is estimated that as many as 75 students per semester may participate in this facet of the program. Senior members of the economics department will rotate responsibilities for the new courses at graduate and undergraduate levels, as is customary, but they will add some computer-based forecasting models and will subscribe to several new periodicals and an on-line data base service. Faculty from all disciplines may nominate potential executives-in-residence, although arrangements for their presence will be made by a coordinator during the program's first two years.

The course on Japanese management style will be open to advanced undergraduates and to students at the graduate level; it will be taught by a member of the psychology department who will need released time for course development. Opening the film series to the public will require additional licensing fees, and adding two art exhibitions per year will mean additional costs for transportation, mounting, security, catalogs, and insurance.

23

The first three years of the International Ventures program will cost approximately $662,000. URC plans to seek endowment for at least one language position, but that will take time. You are looking for corporate and foundation grants to cover the major portion of the cost. You will be writing a proposal to Worldwide Computer, Inc., for a grant of $351,899 to pay for the major portion of the curriculum development. You will also be approaching the Jane and Alfred Bigbucks Foundation for $18,000 for the Art of India exhibit, and the Bell and Whistle Charitable Trust for $68,572 for the language laboratory.

What will it cost?

At the end of this chapter (see page 33), I've included four budgets, based on the University of River City's new international program. *Budget 1: International Ventures Program Costs* would be the first budget you'd develop, but it's not what you'd finally send to Worldwide Computer, Inc. It's an internal planning document, the sort of thing that would be shared with anyone involved in designing or approving plans for the international program. It's detailed, and it covers a three-year period because establishing a program as complex as this one would take at least that long. The folks at URC need to be aware of what funds are required over the period of implementation. To develop this budget you would need to work with quite a few people on campus.

Personnel

Personnel costs are usually the biggest portion of a project budget, and they can sometimes be difficult to establish. It's easy enough to get average current salary figures from the dean of faculty or the business office, and average benefit figures from personnel, but when you ask for projections you may think you've run into a stone wall. People understandably feel that they may have to live with any figures they give you, and you may have to reassure them that the budget can be changed to reflect actual figures when those are established. For the foreign language positions, the budget assumes that the average starting salary for an assistant professor is $21,500, and that full-time faculty will get 6 percent increases in salary in each of the next two years. Benefits, currently at an average of 9 percent of salary for the assistant professor (pre-tenure) level, will increase to 10 percent of salary in Year 2 and remain at 10 percent in Year 3. Note, however, that since the salaries increase in Year 3, the total for benefits increases also.

The history department is getting a part-time person to teach three courses a year, and you'll find that part-time salaries often run substantially below those of full-time personnel. At URC the payment per course is currently $3,100, a number you'd obtain from the dean of faculty's office or the business office. Since URC is concerned about the discrepancy between the earnings of part-time and full-time faculty—the AAUP chapter is extremely active—the trustees have already agreed to increase per course payments regularly over the next several years. The only benefit applied to part-time faculty is the FICA (Social Security) payment for which the institution is liable, and that figure is established by the federal government. Someone in personnel can certainly tell you what it is and whether any increase is planned.

One member of the psychology department will have released time (RT) from one course during the program's first year to develop the new course on Japanese psychology. At URC the policy is to figure RT at the replacement rate—what it would cost to hire a part-time person to teach the course. Another way to find the RT cost is to figure that faculty members are expected to teach six courses per year, so released time equals one-sixth of the individual's salary and benefits. But URC is already committed to the full-timer's support, so the only extra cost is the replacement's salary. (Find out what the policy is at your institution; sometimes the cost of the project director is figured at a percentage of his or her earnings and benefits, whereas other faculty participants are budgeted at the released time figure.)

No faculty member ever wants to coordinate a major new program as an overload. There's a lot of work involved in setting up anything as elaborate as URC's international effort; it will take a good deal of running around, talking to people, making sure deadlines are met, coordinating schedules, and simply being the person to whom questions and suggestions are directed. The cost sheet therefore includes an allowance for a coordinator. Whether an institution chooses to hire someone or release a current faculty member from a course or two will depend on the project and the availability of interested, qualified personnel. This budget indicates that a new person will be hired part time and paid at the released time rate. The project's designers think that less coordination will be needed by the second year, and by the third year the program should be so firmly in place as part of the regular curriculum that there'll be no need for a coordinator.

Finding all those international internships is going to put quite a burden on the placement staff. During development of the program it became obvious that the placement staff will need to add a permanent half-time position, so the budget reflects this. It also includes provision for secretarial support to handle the additional correspondence, reports, and other paperwork that the project will generate, at least during the coordinator's tenure. Projected salary increases for administrative and hourly personnel (the placement appointment and the secretary) are less than those for the teaching faculty.

Secretarial support can be a bone of contention between administrators, faculty members, and clerical staff. No one likes to do extra work without extra time or money, so unless you've thought the matter through during the development of the project, you may find that the paperwork is being passed around like a hot potato once the project is underway. As the proposal writer, you shouldn't make any judgments about how much people should be expected to do, but you should raise the question and be sure that the planners agree, during the planning stage, on how secretarial support will be provided. Make a note for the file; you'll be able to refer to it later, not so you can assign responsibility but so those carrying out the project can remember what was agreed upon. It won't eliminate difficulties, but it may remove some tension.

One of the strengths of this project is the way it involves students as active participants in running the program. Students working as peer tutors in the language programs or as security guards at the gallery exhibitions will learn a great deal, as well as earn money they can put towards college costs. Their hourly rates may well vary depending on their class year and previous campus work experience. Rates are usually based on what the institution pays students qualified for College Work/Study jobs. (Check with your director of financial aid to establish the appropriate rates.) This budget assumes that the peer tutors are juniors or sophomores and that the security guards are seniors or experienced juniors. It also assumes that the rates, which are set by the federal program, won't change in Year 2 but will increase in Year 3.

Your institution may well have a standard honorarium for "normal" guest speakers (although the sky may be the limit for big names). The office of the dean of faculty can probably supply that information.

Equipment and facilities

Developing costs for renovations is an art in itself, but fortunately you don't have to be an expert. The person responsible for the physical plant (the vice president for business, the director of physical plant, or whatever the title) will supply those figures, which are shown in more detail in *Budget 4: Language Laboratory Renovation* (see page 38). You need to be aware of those details and tie them to what you know about the project so that you can ask good questions. For example, the chair of the language department mentions in one of the project development meetings that he's investigating tape players that can play videotapes. Are those the models for which the cost is shown, or did he decide to stick with traditional tape players? Or perhaps the language department decided to go with the new videotape players but no one has told the director of physical plant. You must resolve these questions.

Determine the timetable for the renovations. How soon can work begin if the proposal is funded? What has to happen before it starts? Do offices or classes need to be relocated? Can the work be done at any time of year, or would it be better to wait until classes are out because of the noise and dust? Will this affect the cost of labor and materials, or is the estimate based on a lag time of seven or eight months? How much time should you allow for delivery of equipment? Who will install it and is that included in the price? What is the warranty period, and what does the warranty include? Are there people on campus who can handle repairs if necessary? Should you include service costs for the equipment after the warranty expires? (With computer equipment, especially, the service costs are substantial.) Not all these questions will have answers that you need to translate into dollars, but many will. And what you learn will improve the proposal.

Books, periodicals, and other resources

These items are often overlooked when changes in the curriculum are being planned. It's a good idea to talk to the librarian during the planning process. Depending on how your institution's educational and general budget is developed, items such as videotapes, periodicals, and books may appear in department budgets or in the library budget. Unless provision is made for increased expenditures, buying books and the like for new programs will mean that there aren't enough funds for other books and periodicals. The librarian can almost always supply prices and projections of price increases, and may also tell you about new sources of information, such as the fictitious Third World Data Service, that could strengthen the program.

The trend in the development of library resources is to purchase the basics and try to borrow esoteric materials that are used infrequently. Institutions that are tied in by computer to OCLC (Online Computer Library Center, Inc.) and statewide systems, such as the LCS (Library Circulation System) in Illinois, are at a decided advantage. If expensive publications can be borrowed, your institution and your students save money. A librarian will be able to find out what's available to borrow, and how likely it is that your students and faculty will be able to get it when they need it. But in return, the librarian may suggest including some extra money in the postage budget; it's expensive to ship books.

This budget assumes that the major expense for language videotapes will come in Year 1, with the department's regular budget absorbing the costs after that. Econometrics software, on the other hand, requires yearly updating and payment of licensing fees; dealers usually supply an estimate. The costs of subscribing to a data service can vary tremendously, so ask the librarian to get a quote from the service you intend to use. When you are budgeting for periodicals, you may want to consider subscribing for three years at a time, although this budget indicates a yearly charge. Year 1 will be the big year for purchasing foreign language books, with minimal expenditures budgeted for Years 2 and 3.

Travel

Everybody loves to travel at someone else's expense, although anyone who spends a lot of time on the road may sometimes wonder what the attraction is. Travel is very expensive, especially the international travel required to set up and supervise internships. Make sure you allow enough money for airfare and living expenses in foreign countries. Consult a travel agent and talk to people who have spent time abroad, not just as tourists but as residents. You may find that a per diem tour allowance doesn't come close to covering the cost of a two-week sojourn in Madrid. For example, you will need to add the costs of laundry and dry cleaning to hotel, meals, and in-city transport so that the intern coordinator can maintain a suitably businesslike appearance while calling on upper-level corporate and government officials. You can't expect the traveler to pick up the cost of flowers for his or her hostess, if that's the local custom, or to pay for messenger delivery of a faculty member's recent book to the contact who arranged a meeting with the head of the Prado.

For student interns, too, travel is expensive. Even if your institution lets those receiving financial aid "take it with them," any foreign program will require up to $2,000 in added expenditures. Most aid recipients also hold down work-study jobs to earn money for books and entertainment, and they won't be able to do that on the foreign program since most countries don't allow foreign nationals to earn wages as interns. So this budget assumes that the institution has (or will set up) a revolving loan fund from which students may borrow a certain amount to offset their travel costs.

Travel for guest lecturers should also appear in your cost sheet. Obviously you can't predict where speakers will come from in Year 2 or 3, nor can you be certain of travel costs. But faculty may be able to give you some idea of the regions most likely to supply your speakers (large cities for business leaders, for instance), and a travel agent could give you an educated guess about round-trip airfare. When the time comes, you may find that many business speakers will pay their own way, or that their companies will do so. If you're considering speakers drawn primarily from the for-profit sector, it's safe to underestimate the cost of each trip. But do make some allowance for speakers' travel; the gallery curator may decide that the very best person to lecture on Indian art should be flown in from New Delhi.

Other costs

Sometimes the "Other" category can be the largest item on your cost sheet. URC's project has two big ticket items, both connected with community outreach: the film series and the expanded gallery program. Film rental charges depend on the organization renting the film and the intended audience. If the renting group is a not-for-profit agency that will show the film only to its members, free of charge, the price is substantially lower than if the group intends to open the showing to all comers and charge admission. URC's plans fall somewhere in between; films will be open to the public, free. Make sure the person in charge of arranging for film rental (the campus entertainment coordinator, assistant director of student services, cultural affairs, or the like) understands what's being planned and gets appropriate quotes from the rental agencies.

The gallery program is going to be expensive, but everyone has decided that it will really draw the community to the university. Art objects are fragile and precious, and therefore it costs a great deal to transport and display them. A comprehensive catalog of the exhibition is a major educational benefit, not just for those who view the collection with catalog in hand but for future generations who see these same objects. Insurance charges recognize the value of the objects, and publicity means that more people will hear about and attend the exhibit.

The figures in the cost sheet were probably supplied primarily by the curator who will be arranging the exhibitions, and they don't include the curator's salary.

Like the full-time faculty member, the curator will be paid regardless of the expanded program so there are no new costs. In the specific proposal for the gallery program, you might want to show how much time the curator will devote to the new shows as an institutional contribution, or you might even ask for a portion of the curator's salary. But this cost sheet shows only new expenses.

Hospitality and entertainment can also be expensive. All those guests are going to have to sleep somewhere and eat something, and the costs will have to be borne by someone's budget. Find out what the usual procedures are. Perhaps VIPs always stay at the president's house. Or perhaps your institution has an on-campus hotel or guest house, as URC does. Find out what the standard charge per night is and build it in. You may find that corporate visitors pay their own way or don't spend the night, but you should be prepared.

Food, too, is an item. Your campus food service can give you average costs per meal for visitors, and unless you know that there will be a fancy dinner (which might appear in a different category), it's safe to use those figures. But build in an inflation factor if you're making projections over several years. Gallery openings traditionally include refreshments, and URC will hold brief receptions in connection with the film series, too. College students are always hungry, and the films will get a better turnout if the word gets around that special food will be served. I'm happy to say that the days of depending on faculty wives to bake and serve are long gone, so you'd better show some provision for buying refreshments.

Then there's the whole matter of office expenses: letterhead, postage, copying charges, telephone, pens, paper, floppy disks, and so forth. Don't ignore this or figure that everyone will chip in for these "nickel-and-dime" items. Copying charges can mount up fast, and so can phone bills. Departments have budgets within which they must operate, and no department chairperson will appreciate receiving a notice from the business office, halfway through the fiscal year, that his or her colleagues have already gone 30 percent over the budgeted amount for copying. Someone has to pay. When you're dealing with an interdisciplinary or multidisciplinary effort, it's especially important to make sure there's a separate account, or earmarked funds in a regular account, because the more departments (academic and administrative) involved, the more opportunities to pass the buck. So be sure to acknowledge those costs.

This program requires URC to spend a good deal for phone, postage, and telex in connection with arranging the international internships and scheduling the speakers. At this point it doesn't matter that the placement office will be accruing most of the telephone charges, or that the curriculum development people will do the most copying. The point is to make provision for the added costs.

Who's going to pay for what?

The next step is to figure out what costs the institution will absorb and which will be requested from the corporation or foundation. Substantial cost sharing by the institution demonstrates commitment to the project. Your institution's willingness to bear a portion of the actual dollar cost, which you reflect in the budget, may be a crucial factor in the corporate or foundation decision. No matter how well you talk about the importance of a project, if you're not willing to put some money behind it, you won't have credibility. And no donor likes to carry the burden alone. Showing that you're approaching other organizations for support for your project can also be helpful.

One way of deciding how to allocate costs is to ask a staff member of the corporation or foundation what the organization will fund. Some foundations will not pay fringe benefits under any circumstances, while others have no problem with that but don't want to hear about the nickel-and-dime items. For a while, IBM grants could not be used to purchase equipment. Some corporations won't pay for foreign travel, and many question consulting fees.

Someone who's been involved with government proposals may raise the matter of your "indirect cost rate." This is a figure established by your institution and the Department of Health and Human Services—it's usually a percent of salaries and wages requested in a proposal—that can be added to the budget you submit with proposals to many federal agencies. It is supposed to cover administrative expenses and usual use of facilities, and in many cases it includes fringe benefits as well. The only foundation I know that will allow you to request costs using this rate is the Alfred P. Sloan Foundation and then only under special circumstances. Many corporations won't allow it either. But you should ask a staff member about costs the organization will cover; there may be some you haven't identified. Don't hesitate to ask. It's a sign of professionalism, not ignorance.

It's better if you are designated the liaison with the foundation or corporate staff member. Even if a faculty member is doing the budget, you're more likely to have the time and knowledge to chase details, and you undoubtedly spend more time in your office than a faculty member does. You can accumulate a list of questions and get the answers in one call, avoiding duplication of effort, saving everyone's time, and preventing the staff member from feeling harassed by phone calls from several different people at your institution.

The Bigbucks proposal

Take a look at *Budget 2: Expanded Gallery Program Budget and Narrative* on page 35. This will accompany the proposal to the Jane and Alfred Bigbucks Foundation. You are requesting a grant of $18,000 to cover the major portion of the cost, and, of course, you've already established the fact that the foundation is very interested in this sort of thing. You can deduce two principles by looking at this budget. The first is, "Absorb costs for which you already have funds," and the second is, "Give the donor the glamorous, big ticket items."

Transporting, mounting, and insuring the art objects may not be glamorous, but it is expensive. The catalog is both expensive and glamorous since you've certainly played on its scholarly value in the proposal, and since it can display the foundation's name prominently (assuming the foundation agrees to publicity). Members of the foundation board would have a special opportunity to meet Dr. Shankar, although you wouldn't mention that in the proposal. This budget gives the foundation the opportunity to make something very exciting happen—to make a big impact on all those people who will come to the exhibit.

URC's share of the costs shown here is quite small, but what you would make clear in the proposal is that the university is supplying space ("...works will be displayed in the university's newly renovated Beaux Arts Gallery"), maintenance, and, most of all, the knowledgeable curator who is going to put the show together. (You might supply the curator's curriculum vitae as an appendix.) It's always a good idea to include a budget narrative, which you can use to explain where some of those funds come from.

The Worldwide proposal

Now look at *Budget 3: Project Costs and Funding* on page 37, which will accompany the proposal to Worldwide. You're asking the company for slightly more than half the cost of the first three years of the program, and it's a hefty sum. (You've probably indicated in the proposal that it can be paid over several years.)

From an institutional perspective, this budget is good but not great. Worldwide will pick up the tab for teaching, including benefits, which are lumped in with salaries here, a procedure you'd follow only after making sure that Worldwide would allow it. Some money for peer tutors will come from the College Work/Study funds. You've already got a number of little funds for speakers, and if the truth be known, URC, like many institutions, doesn't really want *more* funds for speakers. It's enough trouble using up what money there is. And it won't be difficult to add a few secretarial hours somewhere.

URC may just have to bite the bullet and pay for a new position in the placement office. That sort of administrative appointment is very hard to raise money for. Like admissions, development, or food service, it's support, and while it's important, it's not as important as teaching. But there may have been quite a struggle before this item got put in the budget.

You'll be going to the Bell and Whistle Charitable Trust for the language laboratory renovations and equipment, a fact you'll mention in the proposal to Worldwide (and vice versa). However, you'd better make sure someone at the Trust knows you're dropping names. In fact, your proposal to the Trust should already have been submitted or be very close to submission. Folks in philanthropy talk to each other, and you don't want the people at the Trust to be looking for a proposal you don't intend to send.

The books, periodicals, and so forth are an integral part of the curriculum revision and a logical item to ask Worldwide to fund. The data service might be especially interesting to Worldwide; you could stress in the proposal that local residents as well as business people in the graduate management programs will have access to it. Someone from Worldwide's marketing division could really make use of it. If that happens you may want to ask Worldwide to pick up its cost after the first three years as well.

Worldwide agreed that the travel of the intern coordinator was an extraordinary expense for the first few years of the program, and its funds could underwrite the cost. Guest lecturers' travel, however, will have to come out of other pockets, probably institutional, since Worldwide doesn't want to pay for the top people at competing companies to visit URC. Your research office has already identified an elderly alumnus, a retired career foreign service officer, who is intrigued by the idea of establishing a travel loan fund that the interns could use.

Although Worldwide isn't interested in art, it is interested in having the film series available for employees and their families. The company will get a little publicity, too, on the posters and flyers that advertise the series.

The cost of hospitality, entertainment, and office expenses will be borne by the university.

With this budget you would certainly attach a detailed narrative that would describe how you arrived at the various figures.

The Bell and Whistle budget

Budget 4: Language Laboratory Renovation (see page 38) is the simplest of all. In the proposal you would describe the International Ventures Program and talk about the cost of the entire project, but there's no need to supply more budget information to the Trust. The Trust staff member has told you that they don't want to have it. Don't even bother with a narrative. However, appendices should include drawings of the space to be renovated and flyers or other material produced by the vendor that describes the console and videotape players.

Budget 1: University of River City
International Ventures Program Costs

	Year 1	Year 2	Year 3	Total
I. Personnel				
Foreign Languages—3 FT				
@ $21,500 (+6%, +6%)	$ 64,500	$ 68,370	$ 72,472	$ 205,342
Benefits @ 9% (+10%, +10%)	5,805	6,386	7,024	19,215
History—1 PT 3 courses				
@ $3,100/course ($3,350,				
$3,500)	9,100	10,050	10,500	29,650
FICA @ 7.1%	646	714	746	2,106
Psychology—RT 1 course	3,100	-	-	3,100
FICA @ 7.1%	217	-	-	217
Coordinator—RT 2 courses				
(1 course)	6,200	3,350	-	9,550
FICA @ 7.1%	434	238	-	672
Placement Office—1 PT @ $9,000				
(+3%, +3%)	9,000	9,270	9,548	27,818
FICA @ 7.1%	639	658	678	1,975
Secretarial Services—5				
hrs/wk x 17 wks x $6/hr				
(+3%, +3%)	510	525	541	1,576
Peer Tutors—11 x 10 hrs/wk x 17				
wks x $3.75/hr ($3.75, $3.90)	7,013	7,013	7,293	21,319
Student Security Guards—12 x 10				
hrs/wk x 8 wks x $4/hr ($4,				
$4.15)	3,840	3,840	3,984	11,664
Honoraria: Guest Lecturers—				
10 x $350	3,500	3,500	3,500	10,500
Total	**$114,504**	**$113,914**	**$116,286**	**$344,704**
II. Equipment, Facilities				
Language Laboratory				
Renovation	29,872	-	-	29,872
Tapemaster	5,700	-	-	5,700
Players—15 @ $2,200	33,000	-	-	33,000
Total	**$ 68,572**	**-**	**-**	**$ 68,572**

(Budget 1 is continued on the next page)

33

Budget 1: University of River City
International Ventures Program Costs
(continued)

	Year 1	Year 2	Year 3	Total
III. Books, Periodicals, Other Resources				
17 Language Tapes	1,275			1,275
Econometrics software (updates)	3,700	275	275	4,250
Third World Data Service	9,200	9,200	9,600	28,000
Periodicals				
Economics	425	425	450	1,300
Languages	940	980	1,100	3,020
Eastern Culture Magazine	1,175	1,250	1,250	3,675
Books (foreign language)	17,527	1,000	1,000	19,527
Total	**$ 34,242**	**$ 13,130**	**$ 13,675**	**$ 61,047**
IV. Travel				
Internship Coordinator	4,500	2,000	2,500	9,000
Guest Lecturers—10 @ $300	3,000	3,000	3,000	9,000
Student Interns (loan fund)	10,000	10,000	10,000	30,000
Total	**$ 17,500**	**$ 15,000**	**$ 15,500**	**$ 48,000**
V. Other				
Film Series	8,000	8,000	8,000	24,000
Gallery Program	33,980	34,000	35,000	102,980
Room and board for corporate speakers, 15 @ $50 ($55, $60)	750	825	900	2,475
Guest Lecturers—10 @ $50 ($55, $60)	500	550	600	1,650
Receptions (gallery, films)	1,000	1,000	1,000	3,000
Phone, postage, telex	1,750	1,800	2,000	5,550
Total	**$ 45,980**	**$ 46,175**	**$ 47,500**	**$139,655**
Grand Total	**$280,798**	**$188,219**	**$192,961**	**$661,978**

Budget 2: Expanded Gallery Program Budget and Narrative
Art of India Exhibit, March-May 1987

	Total Cost	Bigbucks Foundation	URC
Transportation of Artifacts	$ 4,700	$ 4,700	

Mounting
   Miniatures (30), $2,740
   Shiva, attendants, $300
	3,040	3,040	

Catalog
   Research, $1,500
   Photography, $1,750
   Printing (5,000), $4,750
	8,000	8,000	

Insurance	1,500	1,500	
Security (student guards) 6 x 10 hrs/wk	960		$ 960

Guest Lecturer
   Honorarium
   Transportation, room and board
	250
	1,000
		750	250
			250

Reception	500		500
Publicity	700		700
Total	**$20,660**	**$18,000**	**$2,660**

(See Budget 2 narrative on the next page)

Budget Narrative

1. The miniatures are extremely fragile and must be shipped air express in specially designed mailpacks, a condition imposed by the owner who is loaning them for the exhibit. The sculpture of Shiva and attendant gods and goddesses weighs more than 1,000 pounds and requires a reinforced and padded crate. It, too, must be shipped by air.

2. The miniatures will be mounted on acid-free backings with special mats and plexiglass covers. Three will be hung so that they can be viewed from both sides.

Displaying the Shiva sculpture requires special lighting and a "cradle" to hold it in position. The traveling case will form the base of the stand so that the sculpture may be viewed at eye level.

3. Research for the catalog will be done by Jane Smith, currently a graduate student at the Art Institute, during the summer of 1986. She will establish the provenance of 17 miniatures and prepare the text for the catalog.

Many of the works have never previously been photographed. The budget allows for color shots of seven miniatures, black and white for the remainder.

The catalog will contain photographs of each object in the show. As it will be the first scholarly record of many of the objects, copies will be sent to the Library of Congress and to a number of museums with substantial collections of Indian art.

4. The collection is valued at close to $5 million, and the university's insurance agency has requested that we take out an additional rider on the institution's basic policy.

5. The gallery will be open for 120 additional hours because of the exhibition, which will require additional guards. Student guards are trained by Campus Security. They are paid $4 per hour, the standard College Work/Study rate for experienced juniors and seniors. Two guards work each shift.

Student guards eligible for College Work/Study funds will be paid from that budget, while others will be paid with college funds.

6. Dr. Ravi Shankar will be the keynote speaker for the opening of the exhibit. He has agreed to come for the university's standard honorarium; however, he must travel from London, where he will be giving a series of lectures and recitals. The university's "Special Guest Fund" will assume the cost of the honorarium and the standard travel allotment of $250, while the grant will cover the additional $750 for transportation.

7. Holding a reception in connection with the opening of an exhibit is standard university practice. We plan a more extensive affair than usual, however, since we assume that Dr. Shankar's lecture will draw a substantial crowd, not only from the university but from the city and suburbs. The university will assume all costs of the reception.

8. Publicity will include posters, radio announcements on local stations and on URC's own classical music station, and a mass mailing of flyers to local alumni, parents, and friends. Mainstream Bank and Trust has offered to include flyers in its February mailing of bank statements; this should reach an additional 15,000 households.

Budget 3: University of River City International Ventures Program
Project Costs and Funding, 1987-1990

	Worldwide	Other	Total
I. Personnel			
Foreign Language	$ 224,557		$ 224,557
History	31,756		31,756
Psychology	3,317		3,317
Coordinator	10,222		10,222
Placement Office		$ 29,793	29,793
Secretarial		1,576	1,576
Peer Tutors		21,319	21,319
Guest Speakers		10,500	10,500
II. Equipment, Facilities			
Language Laboratory			
Renovation		29,872	29,872
Equipment		38,700	38,700
III. Books, Periodicals, Other Resources			
Tapes	1,275		1,275
Software	4,250		4,250
Data Service	28,000		28,000
Periodicals	7,995		7,995
Books	19,527		19,527
IV. Travel			
Internship Coordinator	9,000		9,000
Guest Lecturers		9,000	9,000
Student Interns		30,000	30,000
V. Other			
Film Series	12,000	12,000	24,000
Gallery Program		114,644	114,644
Hospitality and Entertainment		7,125	7,125
Office Expenses		5,550	5,550
Total	**$351,899**	**$310,099**	**$661,978**

Budget 4: University of River City
Language Laboratory Renovation

Architects' Fees	$ 4,290
Building Permits and Fees	1,725
Electrical Systems	
Cables, boxes, parts	750
Indirect lighting	1,120
Wallboard, Ceiling Tile	690
Carpeting	850
Cabinetry (custom)	9,127
Tapemaster	5,700
Tape Players—15 @ $2,200	33,000
Labor	11,320
Total	**$68,572**

Chapter 4

Writing the Proposal

Y ou've collected lots of data and sorted it into categories. Now you need to begin putting it in logical order. An outline is the most useful way to arrange your material and will help you produce a convincing proposal. It enables you to design a document that will lead the reader inexorably from your premise to your conclusion. An outline will give form to your thoughts; it will help you write well.

An outline can be as detailed or as simple as you care to make it. Its complexity will depend on such things as the nature of your project or need, your own familiarity with the project, and the requirements of the organization to which you are submitting the request. Sometimes the foundation or corporation provides you with a detailed list of the information it wants to see in a proposal. In that case, you're in luck; use the list to sort your information. Put your facts in the order they're asked for and answer all the questions. Staff members have reasons for wanting that information, not just an arbitrary desire to make applicants complete an obstacle course. The organization probably has specific procedures for handling requests, and breaking the rules may derail your proposal. When people are under pressure—and all organizations that make grants are overwhelmed with proposals these days—they tend to put aside things that fall outside normal procedures and are thus harder to handle. You don't want your proposal set aside until someone has time to deal with it. That time may never come or may come too late for the deadlines you are trying to meet.

When you're not lucky enough to be handed a ready-made form, you'll have to develop your own. Regardless of the nature of your request, your outline will contain several basic elements:

I. Introduction
   A. The problem
   B. Your plan
   C. The amount of your request

II. Project description
   A. More about the problem
      1. What's wrong (and how do you know)?
      2. Why is it important to solve the problem?
   B. How you're going to solve the problem
      1. What you're going to do
      2. What others have done
      3. Why your way is better
   C. What it will take to solve the problem
      1. People
      2. Other resources
      3. Money
   D. How you'll know you've solved the problem
      1. What you want to accomplish
      2. What you'll do next
   E. Why your institution is a great place to solve the problem
      1. What you've done in the past
      2. What's happening now
      3. What you're contributing to the solution (talent, time, space, money)
   F. Why a grant from them to you would be especially appropriate
      1. Relationship
      2. Mutual rewards

III. Conclusion
   A. Summary
   B. Thanks

IV. Appendices
   A. Budget and narrative
   B. Specific information
   C. General information

Form: The letter proposal, the formal proposal and the cover letter

You're ready to start writing. But are you going to begin your proposal by saying (in the person of your president), "Dear Mr. Jones: On behalf of the Board of Trustees of Smalltown College, I write to request a grant..." ? Or will you adopt an impersonal tone, forgoing the use of the first person entirely? Whether you choose to draft a letter proposal or a formal proposal, which will be accompanied by a more personal cover letter, depends on several factors:

- the complexity of the project or program you will be describing;
- the existing relationship between your institution and the organization receiving the request; and
- the requirements of the organization to which you are sending the proposal.

It is always best to follow the instructions provided by the foundation or corporation you are approaching. If the organization furnishes a list of questions that should be answered in the proposal, you have probably used it to collect and organize information. You may well have based your outline on the order in which those questions were asked. If so, you can begin to construct the narrative for your proposal with confidence.

Some agencies don't want a flowing narrative. The Joyce Foundation, for example, has a detailed questionnaire divided into sections covering various aspects of an institution. Following that outline does not produce a coherent, linked narrative, but it does give staff members the information they need to assess your institution's capacity to do whatever it is you are proposing. The Brunswick Foundation asks that the answer to each of five questions begin on a separate page, so that different reviewers can consider specific sections without having to examine the entire proposal. This means that your answer to question 4 ("What is the greatest problem facing higher education today, and how does your institution deal with it?") is being judged against all the other replies to that question, outside the context of any other information about your institution. This poses some special problems about what to include. Essentially, you have to describe your institution's special strengths in each answer, not merely once in the entire proposal.

Don't try to short-circuit the process. If an organization has put together a numbered list of questions, it's quite likely that a staff member goes through every proposal and checks to see that each question has been answered. If you haven't provided an answer, it may count against you; if your answer is obscure, that person may not have the leisure to search for it. If, for instance, you're asked to state the amount of grant aid that your institution is providing to students from its own resources, supply that figure and make sure it's clearly labelled. Don't make the staff member break it out from the total dollars budgeted for aid, including federal and state support.

A corporation or foundation will often request specific information without dictating the form in which that information should appear. When you are well along in the drafting process—before you are ready to send the proposal out to those on campus who need to review it—go over it once more to be sure that you have supplied all the information somewhere in the draft and that it is easy to find.

The letter proposal

Foundation or corporation guidelines for the submission of a proposal often say nothing about the form they prefer or say that there is no preferred form. Then you must consider the other two criteria to decide what form to use: your institution's relationship to the granting organization and the complexity of your project. Focus on the people who will be reading your proposal. What do they need to know in order to respond to your request? If you are drafting a proposal to a local foundation that has previously made grants to your institution for financial aid to assist local students, you might put the request in the form of a letter from your president to the president, executive director, or head of the foundation. The people in charge of making grants already know a great deal about your institution; you're not going to have to use a lot of paper describing its mission, goals, strategies, resources, accomplishments, personnel, and needs. You don't have to dwell on "Why us?" although you'll certainly want to refer to your institution's strengths and recent achievements. In this case, you can justify the need for financial aid quite briefly; basically, you're trying to help qualified individuals make the most of their talents for the benefit of society as a whole. This proposal, therefore, could take the form of a letter of two to three pages. It might be organized as follows:

Dear (first name):

Reference to recent meeting or contact; transition to request for [amount] for scholarships for local students; reference to previous similar support.

Update on campus situation: general statement of well-being, mention of items of specific interest to reader, appropriate references to current faculty, student accomplishments. Achievements of past recipients of foundation aid.

Transition to current increase in enrollment, especially of local students; increased need for student support resulting from changes in federal and state funding. Aid budget; percent of increase. Importance of continued support from individuals and organizations. Long-term plans for funding aid.

Reiteration of request, value of past support. Offer of further information, meeting. Statement of intention of writer to contact reader.

Cordial close,
(first name).

Appendices: table showing five-year growth in number of local students enrolled, number receiving assistance; total aid budget and where it comes from; current auditors' report; list of current trustees; list of recent grants from local corporations and foundations; copy of article reviewing book written by former foundation scholarship recipient.

A typical letter proposal will be handled in this fashion. While it still contains answers to the questions described in Chapter 2, many are brief because the reader is already well-informed about your institution. Under no circumstances, however, should you neglect to provide those answers. One of the dangers of the letter proposal is that you begin to assume too much knowledge on the part of the reader, and as a result you fail to provide justification for your request. Be sure to state the need (in this case, educated young people) in framing your appeal. Put the amount of your request in the context of institutional finances. Show that a grant will make a difference.

Avoid overfamiliarity. A letter proposal is not personal correspondence. In almost every case, the person to whom the letter proposal is addressed will share it with the others involved in deciding whether to make a grant to your institution. Be certain that the proposal is one which he or she can show with pride. Don't embarrass the reader; supply enough information, and the right sorts of information, so that a grant becomes a way of helping your institution achieve some goals of concern to the foundation or corporation. Don't make it appear that a grant in answer to your proposal would be an indulgence of the reader's hip-pocket charities.

It's a little different when you approach a small family foundation or a business whose shares, if it's set up that elaborately, are all held by members of the family. The family business might be the local drycleaner, real estate agency, manufacturing concern, or restaurant. A successful appeal to the owner may well generate a check on a company account. Legally, this is a corporate contribution, just as the check from the Ethelyne Smith Family Trust is a grant from a family foundation. But functionally these are contributions from individuals. The donors are solicited as individuals; they answer only to themselves in the matter of contributions and have complete autonomy in deciding where their philanthropic interests lie. And your institution often acknowledges this by making them members of giving clubs and providing the sorts of recognition offered to other generous individuals. Any proposal you draft in this case is likely to be distinctly informal and aimed at advancing the interests of the individual, not the foundation or corporation.

Generally, a letter proposal shouldn't be much longer than two to two and one-half pages. The first page is necessarily short because the recipient's name and addresss, the salutation, and the letterhead (top and bottom) take up space. Page two (and be sure to number your pages) could be the one "full" page, while page three should be less than completely full. That much single-spaced prose won't strain the reader's eyes and should give you plenty of time to make the crucial points. If you find that your planned letter proposal is turning out to be longer than that, you should think about making it into a formal proposal with cover letter or supplying some of the information in attachments. You may well have more to say than you can fit into a letter or you may have let the argument run away with you. In that case, cut.

Proposal writers at small institutions may find that the letter proposal is the president's preferred form for most corporate and foundation solicitations. This is not only because smaller institutions undertake relatively few projects of great magnitude but because, very often, the president has already established a relationship with the individual being addressed, and calls on this relationship to give credibility to the request. If you work for a small institution you should be aware of this habit, if it exists, and be ready to suggest the use of the most appropriate tone (and form) for each recipient. Don't hesitate to draft a formal proposal if the subject matter requires it or if corporation or foundation guidelines dictate a specific format. All the advantages of the letter proposal can be gained in other ways.

The formal proposal

What form is most appropriate if you are drafting a request to Worldwide Computer for a major grant to help the University of River City establish its new international thrust? This is a complex program with many facets, and justifying the need for this program, spelling out reasons why URC is a good place to set it up, describing the many steps to be taken, and explaining the costs involved will surely require more than three pages. In addition, such a proposal will most likely be acted on by a group of individuals with little prior knowledge of URC. You will need to provide general background and to describe specific strengths in which the corporation might wish to invest. This request demands a formal proposal.

Your outline is now invaluable. You will be grappling with a mass of material; you will need to sort the relevant from the trivial, link concepts with actions, and impose convincing order on something that may not be very well ordered in the minds of its proposers. You will have to describe in linear fashion ("first we will do this, then that, then the other") the seemingly amorphous mass of the project, in which a great many things are happening simultaneously. And you have to do it so that the readers don't get distracted by any one aspect of the project. Good organization is crucial to your success, and your outline can ensure that you stay organized. It will help you construct a case that will lead the readers from your premise, which is that your institution can do something of interest to the corporation, through a tightly reasoned series of justifications for your request, to a conclusion. In most cases, you will assemble your narrative along the following lines:

Introduction: brief statement of problem (lack of college graduates trained to deal with international concerns); your solution (international relations curriculum) and why your institution is qualified to provide it (tradition of international involvement); total cost; amount of request.

Developed description of problem/need in context appropriate to Worldwide: growth in international trade, competition from foreign markets, new plants to River City, need for trained employees, community acceptance; how problem is apparent nationally (reference to national commission report; enrollments in foreign languages down, insularity up among students; no knowledge of geography).

History of URC as it relates to your recognition of problem and ability to solve it: strong language faculty, existing international relations major, popularity of business major and graduate programs; tradition of domestic internships, close ties with local business community, new interest in Japanese business; new gallery curator.

Description of International Ventures Program: curriculum revision committee's task, membership; goal of program (prepare more individuals to understand and deal with international issues, organizations); specific objectives (graduate more students to careers in international business; provide management training in international business; provide opportunities for community to become more familiar with other cultures); methods (require foreign language training, international culture course for undergraduates; overseas internship program; add international economics courses; develop intercultural sequence; open foreign film series and offer more art exhibits); needs (personnel in languages, placement; released time for course development; books, periodicals; speakers).

Who's in charge: credentials of project director, those most closely involved. Timetable: first course offered, internships begin, dates of art exhibitions, adoption of language and culture course requirements.

Evaluation: how many majors, interns, graduate students; attendance at films, exhibits; careers. General projections for next decade.

Costs: total cost, how much institution plans to absorb, where other funds are being sought, long-term plans for funding program. Institution's current financial health; other grants received recently. Other related success.

Conclusion: how success of program will assist Worldwide, other multinationals, community, students. How Worldwide's support is critical to success of program: funds, recognition, respectability, leadership gift, timeliness, neighborly relationship between Worldwide and URC, Worldwide's concern for community. Offer of additional information, with contact names and phone numbers.

Appendices: budget and narrative; schedule of program development; credentials of principal faculty; local corporations and numbers of middle management people from each enrolled in graduate business program; internship enrollments (five-year growth) and list of sponsors; audited financial statement; current list of trustees; IRS Letter of Determination; current URC budget; Fact Sheet.

How long should a proposal be? The classic answer to this question is "as long as necessary to make your case." When a foundation or corporation has set limits, you should certainly abide by them, although I have never known a proposal to be disqualified because its final paragraph and the president's signature were on a third page and guidelines called for no more than two pages. But I'd think long and hard before sending a five-page proposal under those circumstances. It's a real test of skill to distill the essence of your institution and the particular concern being addressed into so few words. But you want your proposal to be read, and unless you follow the rules you can't guarantee it will be.

You can gain a little space by adopting the formal proposal form. You can also single-space your formal proposal or make the margins of your letter proposal a little narrower than usual. However, these tricks may backfire. Your proposal will look crowded and messy, thus making your institution look less than thoroughly professional. Remember, it's not a contest; you're not trying to fool the foundation or corporation staff member into reading a few more words from your institution than from the competition. You are trying to get the reader on your side, and anything that smacks of manipulation leaves a bad impression of your institution and diminishes your proposal's chance of success.

A formal proposal can be almost any length, from two to 20 pages (and I have known some longer than that). But it's preferable to keep it short. You and your colleagues on campus may be fascinated with every detail of your project, but how much do you think someone at a corporation or foundation *really* needs to read in order to be persuaded of the virtues of your plan? Even with a table of contents, headings, and carefully numbered appendices to help the reader sort through the mass of paper you've sent, there are still a lot of pages to shuffle. And yours is not the only proposal being considered. Make it memorable, not confusing. If you conclude with the names and telephone numbers of contact people, the reader can get more information if they need it.

The cover letter

With the formal proposal you will almost always send a cover letter. Coming from the president or ranking person at your institution, the cover letter is your chance to get personal, to refer to the donor's self-interest more directly than would be appropriate in the formal proposal, to reiterate aspects of the relationship between your institution and the organization being approached, to praise the project staff, to cite endorsements of the project by individuals known to the recipient, and to mention matters that don't fit neatly into the proposal but that concern the reader.

The cover letter also contains a one- or two-line summary of the project or purpose, including the amount being requested, even though the proposal contains this information and the organization may have requested that you send a separate "summary sheet." Strange things have been known to happen to proposals, some inadvertent and some by design. What left your office as a carefully assembled document consisting of cover letter, summary sheet, proposal, typed appendices, catalog, and printed brochure may end up in pieces in five different locations at the corporation or foundation. You don't want anyone to spend time wondering what your president is requesting money for this time, or just how much money your institution needs to carry out the terrific idea that is described in the proposal but, unfortunately, doesn't seem to have a price tag, because the cost is mentioned only in the cover letter.

A cover letter to accompany the proposal to Worldwide Computer might be structured as follows:

> Dear (first name):
>
> Reference to their discussion at most recent Chamber of Commerce subcommittee meeting; how project·described in attached proposal reflects those mutual concerns.
>
> Description of project, time frame, total cost, amount being requested from Worldwide.

Critical importance of Worldwide support to institution, students, community, multinational business. Praise for similar efforts that demonstrate Worldwide's foresight, generosity.

Offer to arrange meetings between URC's key project people, Worldwide's top brass, and/or key staff. Promise to follow up.

Cordial close,
(first name)

Your president may know their top person and send the proposal directly to him or her. Or the cover letter might be addressed to the individual in charge of philanthropy at the corporation or the executive director of the foundation, if that is the person with whom your president has developed a relationship. Or it might go to whomever the organization has named to receive correspondence. Sometimes, too, the top person tells your president (or the executive director tells you) to address the cover letter or the letter proposal to the designated staff member regardless of the relationship between your president and the head of the organization. Don't try to circumvent such specific instructions because you think your proposal will get better treatment if it goes to the office of the chair of the board. You'll actually lose points for "bad manners," and you may also lose time. Who knows how long the proposal will sit in someone's IN basket before it finally goes to the right office?

There is a way to use presidential clout (yours or theirs) when you've got it: Send the proposal and cover letter (or letter proposal) to the office as instructed, but on the letter (or letter proposal) indicate that a copy is going to the top person at the foundation or corporation. You should explain somewhere in your cover letter or letter proposal that the person being copied is a graduate (or whatever the connection may be). In that case, putting "cc: Daddy Bigbucks" on your proposal is almost as effective as addressing it to Bigbucks himself. But do it only if you know that Bigbucks is willing to appear to be sponsoring your appeal.

Style

As writers, our moment of truth comes when we realize we've got to stop gathering information and start producing a coherent, convincing document. This can be terrifying. People develop different ways of overcoming their fear of the blank page (or computer monitor). Some jump into the middle of the proposal and begin by describing the program or purpose; others labor intensely over an opening sentence. Some, realizing that they'll be rewriting it all anyway, just start throwing words at the paper. Whatever method you adopt, the easiest way to organize your words is to use your outline. It's the skeleton of your proposal, and if you keep it in front of you, you'll be able to create a unified, persuasive document.

The words you choose and the order in which you use them produce a tone that can add immeasurably to the impact of your proposal or can diminish or even contradict the messages you are trying to convey. To ensure that your writing reinforces your request, consider your reader; consider your material; consider your goal—what you want to accomplish with your writing. Then apply the various elements of style. You hope to persuade the reader not only to read through your proposal but to do something after he or she finishes reading. You want the reader to undertake a series of actions (causing other people to read your proposal, to consider the ideas, and to decide to support them) that culminate in your institution's achievement of a particular goal.

If you focus on the reader, you will find that your style changes with each proposal. Even if you are writing several proposals requesting funds for the same purpose, the proposals will differ because your institution's relationship with each grant-making organization differs. No matter what your proposal is about, whether you're dealing with an art program, a new field house, financial aid for Native Americans, or a chair in economics, you should be conscious of what concerns this specific reader and what he or she needs to know. People who assume there is one specific style of proposal writing are either insensitive or they are looking for a magic formula, which they won't find.

The best proposals bear no imprint of the proposal writer. If you want to display your talent for creative writing, try the great American novel or a sonnet sequence—on your own time. The creativity involved in proposal writing revolves around a sensitivity to nuance, the ability to draw conclusions about interest and character on the basis of limited material, and the ability to synthesize and describe, clearly and convincingly, the ideas of many people. You create a document that articulates others' concerns and builds on the relationship between your institution and the organization being approached.

The following sections cover some aspects of style as they pertain directly to proposal writing. A substantial number of factors go into good writing, and I'm not going to attempt to deal with them all here. For specific guidance, read (and reread) Strunk and White's *Elements of Style,* Fowler's *Modern English Usage,* and Zinsser's *On Writing Well* (see bibliography). For general assistance, *read.* Train your eye to examine any writing, from the copy on a cereal box and the direct mail letter addressed to Occupant to the latest novel or guide to nonprofit management. As you read, try to figure out what the writer intended to do, whether it worked, and why it succeeded or failed. Be critical. And be ready to turn the same objective eye on your own writing.

Tone

Pronouns give you an obvious opportunity to reflect a relationship in the proposal and to strengthen whatever special reasons you have for sending this particular request to this particular organization. Any use of the first and second person pronouns ("I," "we," "you") in a proposal implies a personal relationship between writer and reader and decreases the distance between them. The letter proposal and the cover letter use this personal approach. Each is written in the first person, and this helps create or draw on the feeling of a personal and preexisting relationship with the recipient.

A tone of intimacy is a special strength of the letter proposal and the prime purpose of the cover letter. Each is an effort to make the request more personal, to move from the abstract into the particular, to tie the concepts described in the proposal to the reality of people. And it can be extremely effective. When properly done, it differentiates your institution and your program from the myriad others being described to the foundation or corporation personnel.

But the personalized approach has its pitfalls. As the proposal writer, you must remember (and impress upon whoever is signing the letter) that even though the document is in letter form, it is not the solicitation of an individual. It doesn't matter whether your president has known Alfred Bigbucks for years, plays golf with him every Wednesday, and is married to his second cousin once removed. Good ol' Al isn't the only person who will read that cover letter or that proposal to the Bigbucks Foundation, and you want him to be proud to share it with the others involved in making a decision about the grant. Don't say anything that might embarrass him. Keep the private jokes out of it; refer to a recent visit to his office or to a professional rather than a personal meeting. Be informal but not casual.

Be sure you've provided enough information. Reflect that in the tone of your letter as well as in the content. Don't assume, implicitly or explicitly, that Al knows everything about what you have in mind, agrees with it, and is just waiting to send you a check. Be very careful about using such phrases as "I'm sure you remember" or "As you know...." While they can sometimes give you an excuse for restating some information that should be included, they are cliches. And if you don't retell what he supposedly knows, Bigbucks may not remember or may be annoyed that you take his memory of the conversation for granted as if your institution's projects are his most pressing concerns. He may have much bigger fish to fry!

Avoid inserting the reader's first name into the letter at intervals. ("It was great to see you, Jane, at the last Garden Club meeting.") With the advent of word processing, every direct mail fund raiser started to use that trick in an effort to make the reader believe that he or she was being personally addressed. It may work in direct mail (although I have my doubts—it's not used nearly as frequently as it used to be), but it backfires in a proposal. You've established the first-name relationship in the salutation, and you should demonstrate the reasons for it in the text. Additional use of the first name is redundant. It's supposed to make a letter sound like speech, but it doesn't work. Instead it sounds like you're trying to manipulate the reader by stressing the personal nature of the relationship, and it focuses on the personal ties between writer and reader rather than on the merits of the proposal itself. Regardless of those ties, this is still a transaction between one organization and another, and the other people involved in the decision will resent any implication to the contrary.

One of the great virtues of the letter form is that it encourages you to write simply. When you're writing a letter it's hard to be pompous. Somehow it's easier to remember that this document is going to be read by a real person. Eliminating the personal pronoun can take all the life out of a formal proposal. Its impersonal style seems turgid at best and at worst so convoluted that it is difficult to figure out exactly what is being requested by whom for what purpose. But it is perfectly possible to maintain a tone that will keep the reader involved even though you are not addressing an individual by name. You do it by focusing your prose on the interests of the reader and reflecting your knowledge of the organization's concerns with key words and phrases. Writing to Worldwide Computer, for instance, you'd mention information technology, international trade, and competition with Japanese manufacturers, and you'd think up several ways of expressing each concept. This proves to the CEO that you've got Worldwide's interests in mind, not just URC's needs. A formal proposal to the Bigbucks Foundation for the gallery program might include references to the need for diversity, intercultural awareness, art as a learning tool, and the importance of educating the community. Direct your prose from the writer to the reader and center it on the reader. It's not enough to be aware of the reader's interests; you've got to make that awareness explicit.

Voice

Just as the letter proposal format can entice you into becoming too casual and intimate, the formal proposal can encourage you to say things so tediously that your reader wants to take a nap before finishing the second page. One of the great culprits is the passive voice: "It was decided...," "Plans have been drawn up...." Passive voice is dull because it's depersonalizing. By using it you throw away the opportunity to convey the sense of real people doing interesting things, one of your strongest selling points. Passive voice is cowardly; you can hide behind it. A formal proposal written primarily in the passive voice conveys contradictory meanings. You are saying that your institution is capable of carrying out this terrific project, but your language implies that no one is responsible. So use active verbs. Your prose, and thus your proposal, will sound capable and confident.

Word choice

Use good words. "Educationalese" is a laughingstock in academic as well as nonacademic circles. People see it as an obvious effort to make something sound more important than it is. Avoid jargon. If you need to describe scientific instrumentation, for instance, or discuss the latest theory of language development, you may use technical terms, but don't pepper your prose with specialized language or acronyms. The reader doesn't want to keep looking back to find out what "CAPHE" stands for or what an "nmr" is. (Of course, if this is a proposal for a new nuclear magnetic resonance spectrometer and it is going from one chemist to another, you can probably get away with using nmr as often as you like.)

Technical language may intimidate, and that won't necessarily produce a grant. Your writing will be much more effective if you follow the term with a definition in lay language or, if it's an instrument, with an explanation of what it does. Your reader will be pleased to have learned something. That's the business of your institution, after all: to teach. If you can write a proposal that teaches the reader something, without oversimplifying or patronizing, you are demonstrating your institution's ability to educate and strengthening your case for support.

Cliches and trendy phrases are the junk food of proposal writing—they provide lots of calories but little nourishment. We all tend to think that certain magic words or phrases will make our proposals so strong that they cannot be denied. We look for—and find—formulas: "I respectfully request consideration," "an excellent education," "an outstanding faculty," "a corporate investment in the best young minds of today." Watch out for that comfortable phrase.

Your writing will be much stronger if you can find a new way to say the same old thing. Maybe you don't need to say it at all. Doesn't the reader know that you are asking to have your request considered? After all, that *is* the purpose of your proposal. You don't need to *say* that your faculty is excellent if you can document their excellence, perhaps by citing recent publications or awards. Remember that the people making giving decisions at those companies see hundreds of proposals, all trying to interest them in "making an investment in higher education" or helping their students prepare for "the real world."

Use words properly. Computer-related terms have been turning up with considerable frequency in proposals over the past few years. Is your institution attempting "to build up its constituent data bases"? If you're talking about increasing the number of applicants, say so. Computerese is useful only if you're discussing computers. "Cutting edge" and "state-of-the-art" are often applied to science programs and needs that, unfortunately, are not even close to those desirable states. "Parameter" and "quantum" have precise meanings; if you use them incorrectly, anyone who knows what they mean will perceive your writing as sloppy, and others will dismiss them as just so much filler.

Be grammatical. "Hopefully" is widely misused. The word is an adverb and should modify a verb. Don't say, "Hopefully, you will send us money" when you mean "We hope you will send us money." Better yet, don't talk about "hope" at all. It's inappropriate in a proposal—it sounds too emotional, too uncertain.

Remember that "presently" means soon; "currently" and "at present" mean now. Spell correctly. "Alot" and "alright" are incorrect; each is two words. Be very careful of "its" (possessive) and "it's" (contraction of "it is").

You may feel that sports metaphors make your proposal more appealing to "the boys" reading it. Perhaps metaphors are colorful, but is your admissions office really making an "end run" around the competition? Do you want to convey the feeling of competition and suspense that are part of sports events: Will we make it or will the other guys win? You don't want to put your own victory in doubt, nor do you want to trivialize what you're trying to do.

You may be tempted to use current management jargon to make it sound as though the people at your institution are just as efficient as the people who run the Fortune 500 companies. Resist the temptation. Don't say, "This college is intensifying its search for diversity in the income stream due to declining enrollments and a competitive marketplace." Grammatical problems aside, this sentence may be trendy but it is almost incomprehensible. "Declining enrollments and increased competition for applicants have forced this college to intensify its search for new sources of income" says it much better. You may have to put your foot down when the people for whom you are drafting the proposal want to be sure that the corporate folks know they've read *Megatrends, In Search of Excellence,* or *Re-inventing the Corporation.* If they've really read those books, they'll respond to your gentle reminder that it's more effective to demonstrate the ways in which your institution meets the various criteria than to state that it does. Using so-called business language doesn't improve the management of your institution or its ability to market itself.

Persuade by force of reason, not by emotion. It's almost impossible to convince a foundation or corporation board to support your project because of nostalgia for those ivy-covered halls. References to the good old days aren't going to influence people who are concerned with today's profit-and-loss statements, unless you are using history to support your claims of current capability and future achievement. Members of the board may be interested in helping you memorialize the company's founder in your new library, but they'll indulge the edifice complex only if the building will promote the company's interest in some way.

Avoid words such as "desire," "wish," "feel," "fear." Remember that you're not dealing with one individual, who might be swayed by an appeal to emotion, but with a group of individuals whose responses might well differ. Responsible managers invest in good management, and if your proposal sounds fearful ("A contribution of $5,000 is absolutely crucial to the success of this important program"), it will convey an image of desperation and poor management. If your institution's total budget is in the millions, and the program is so important, why haven't you come up with the money before this?

You don't want to sound tentative either. "Perhaps you could consider..." is a formula often used by those requesting major gifts from individuals, and perhaps the asker and the potential donor consider it more comfortable than a direct request. But in a proposal, that language conveys uncertainty. You've done your homework, and you know that your request is reasonable; don't weaken it. When people are giving other people's money away, they need justification for their decisions. Give them confident prose, reflecting a strong institution.

Let your words and the order you put them in convey emotion. Don't use exclamation points. They convey *your* emotion, which may not be shared by the reader. Underlining is another emotional statement that loses its impact with time and distance. You're constructing a document to be read, not a speech to be delivered. Just as the dullest speeches are those read from a prepared text, what's effective verbally loses much of its punch on paper.

Modifiers

Keep your prose as simple as possible. This isn't easy; we all tend to clutter up our writing. Maybe we feel it sounds more important if we use more words or longer words or special words. Or maybe we think weight is impressive. For those of us whose training in writing is primarily academic rather than journalistic, there's another trap. Academic writing tends to be long-winded; it's almost a law of nature that you never say anything once if you can say it four times. There are two reasons for this: First, a prime purpose of academic writing is to convince the reader how much the writer knows, rather than persuade the reader that the writer can do something to advance the reader's interests. Second, most academics spend more time conveying information orally than putting it in writing. When you're lecturing you need to repeat yourself, so that the listeners who didn't catch it the first time have another chance. The reader, on the other hand, can reread the second paragraph if necessary.

Adjectives are clutter and, like all qualifiers, tend to weaken rather than strengthen your statement. Use them only if they will add to the reader's knowledge in a way important to the success of your request. Telling the reader that average SAT scores of entering freshmen have climbed from 1050 to 1126 is impressive; referring to your "increasingly well-qualified, capable students" without supplying the statistics is not. Every institution has increasingly well-qualified, capable students. If you refer to your facilities as "the finest chemistry laboratories in the country," you'd better be able to document it. Be careful of claims to excellence, uniqueness (neither word *ever* takes a modifier), and superiority. It's all too easy for a foundation or corporation staff member to disprove your claims, and your institution loses credibility in direct proportion to the degree of puffery in your prose.

Adjectives are distracting. If you're opening the proposal with a request for money to renovate your *historic* theater, you'd better be renovating it because of its value as a historic building rather than its importance to aspiring actors. The reader will be waiting for descriptions of its architectural merit and its value as a monument to the past. If the real case is that the renovation is going to serve today's students in an important way, you may want to mention that it's the oldest building on campus, but that's not your main point.

You may find it helpful at times to go through your draft and cross out all your adjectives. If it doesn't make sense without them, you need to rewrite, using stronger nouns and verbs. Make sure you've defined your terms. A reference to the excellence of your library may have a clear meaning to those on campus, but if you're counting on your use of special book storage to save space or your unusual data base searching service to impress that foundation executive, you'd better describe it in more detail.

Avoid modifiers such as "quite," "very," "too," and "rather." Show why something is "truly important"; saying it is doesn't make it so. Would you ever ask for something truly unimportant? (Or admit it in print?) Don't use "in a very real sense." That's garbage. Say "now," not "at this point in time." "Needless to say" is just that.

Transitional words and phrases help the reader move easily through your prose and give your writing a sense of flow and balance. "But" is one of the strongest; it tells the reader that you are going to introduce a new and contradictory idea. Others include "yet," "however," "still," "therefore," "thus," "as a result," and all the ways of listing without using a list: "The effects included, first...second...." But beware of too many numbers; a long list gets boring. And watch out for that many-handed Indian god. You may find yourself writing, "On one hand..., on the other hand..., on the third hand...."

Revising and editing

Very few of us can produce a beautifully written proposal in one draft. Learning to rewrite your own and other people's work is almost as important as learning to do the draft in the first place. The key to revising is objectivity.

Editing someone else's work is considerably easier than revising your own drafts. You come fresh to another person's writing, which makes it easier to spot grammatical mistakes, redundancies, lapses in logic, and even typographical errors. Since you don't have a personal interest in someone else's words, it doesn't hurt to eliminate or change them. But before you begin using your red pen, be sure you understand the objectives of the proposal, the requirements of the organization that will be receiving it, and the nature of the individuals who will be reading it. As you edit, keep yourself focused on those basic factors so that you can make sure the proposal itself is properly focused.

It takes tact to edit well. There is no perfect writing style, so be sure your "corrections" are improvements, not mere changes to a style with which you are more comfortable. If possible, ask the person who created the draft why he or she used a particular phrase or organized the material in a certain fashion. Be willing to listen; together, you may find a more effective way of making a point. Perhaps you're trying to train a new staff person or you're working with a faculty member. These are people with whom you want to maintain a good working relationship, and implying that they're terrible writers won't improve their skills or help you get this proposal in the mail. Be patient, don't patronize, and try to explain why you think that certain changes will improve the document.

Editing your superior can be especially tricky, particularly if the president, dean, or "ranking officer" fancies his or her writing skills. Rare is the CEO who takes kindly to the implication that substantial revisions will improve something he or she has drafted. At some level any suggestions will always rankle. The safest and most honest tack to take is the need to focus on the requirements of the foundation or corporation that will receive the proposal. Try to persuade your boss to confine the personal style to the cover letter or to the opening and closing paragraphs of the letter proposal. And be sympathetic; being edited is the hardest task of all, and you don't enjoy it either. Your ego is on the line, and while you have to grow a thick skin to be a writer at all, it takes an extra measure of self-confidence to produce a document that will be critiqued by several people on campus before being put to the ultimate test. Keep your eye—and your president's eye—on the goal of getting a grant.

Revising your own work demands a special kind of strength. You have to pretend that you've never seen it before, and you have to be ruthless. When you see "We are currently engaged in planning for a major capital campaign designed to increase the endowment," don't get swept along by the rhythm; cut. "We are planning a capital campaign to increase the endowment" says it all. You don't need three involvement words ("engaged," "planning," "designed") where one will do. You can plan; you don't have to plan for, except for the future. Capital campaigns are major by definition; using both words is redundant. And the present tense of your verb ("are planning") eliminates the need for "currently."

Learn to recognize your own faults and guard against them. I tend to overwrite and have to force myself to cut. Someone I often edited (and vice versa) is a comma freak and will insert them wherever a speaker might pause for breath. A friend who got started in journalism tells a great story, but finds it hard to put in the actual request for money. Another friend has written a great many proposals for government agencies and has difficulty defining concepts in words of less than four syllables. We all have bad habits, but it's possible to overcome them.

Maintaining objectivity is easier if you can put a draft aside for a few days or even a few hours. You come back to it with a fresh eye. A colleague will never rush revisions so that a proposal can go out at the end of the day; rereading it in the morning provides a last chance to spot errors, without the 5 o'clock pressure of secretaries' and express mail deadlines. It's a good idea to ask someone who is not involved with the project to read your draft. If that person has difficulty understanding parts of it, you need to rewrite.

When you've worked with faculty members to develop a project, you'll probably want to ask them to check the draft for accuracy. (Sometimes they must approve it.) This can produce interesting results. I've gotten reactions ranging from awe (rare) to major rewrites (also rare, fortunately). A faculty member who subjected me to the latter commented that a proposal should be so gloriously written that the recipient should want to read it several times. That rewrite would have required considerable rereading. The prose was glorious, but almost incomprehensible. My response was that the pressure on foundation and corporation staff members these days is so great I want to be sure that they'll only *need* to read it once.

Sometimes suggestions for revisions contradict each other. Obviously you need to adopt the suggestions made by the most knowledgeable person: the computer expert, if you're requesting funds for hardware, or someone in the admissions office if the subject is numbers of applicants. Occasionally the revisers are confusing apples and oranges: "Aid from college resources" may include state capitation grants for the business officer, while the director of financial aid doesn't count them because his office doesn't administer them. Be sure the data you use are what you intend. It's surprisingly easy for an inaccuracy to creep into your proposal. If the president refers to the 11.5 percent increase in the number of transfer students, you're likely to assume the number is correct. But presidents, too, are prone to hearing lapses, and if your use of that figure in the draft comes back with a large question mark from the dean, you'd better check with admissions.

Errors of substance are unavoidable, and your hope is that those who read the draft will be knowledgeable and thorough enough to catch and correct them. Errors of style are another matter entirely. We all know committees can't write; they can't edit either. Look over any suggestions and use those that correct grammatical or spelling mistakes. Ignore the others if you can, though you may have to follow the suggestions of the person who will sign the proposal even if you don't agree with them, unless you can convince him or her that they're not necessary. In the case of conflicting suggestions you'll have to go with those of the ranking person.

Boilerplate

Do we recycle prose? Of course! It's the rare proposal that doesn't require some general description of your institution, and you certainly should develop one all-purpose statement that can be plugged in as needed. But use those processed paragraphs with care. Before you insert them, consider the main points you're trying to make in the proposal and revise with an eye to the reader's interests. Your boilerplate may mention enrollment, student-faculty ratio, the degrees you offer, your library, your endowment, your operating budget, and how much you're spending on financial aid. If you're writing to a corporation interested in minorities, you may well want to mention in that descriptive paragraph that 12 percent of your students are black and 3 percent are Hispanic. A foundation may be totally uninterested in minorities and care about the number of books and periodicals in the library. Pick and choose thoughtfully.

When you use boilerplate, be sure it's up-to-date. Has the enrollment changed? Has the operating budget or the endowment increased? After the books close don't forget to change your phrase about approaching the end of the fiscal year. And have you come closer to reaching your capital campaign goal?

Watch out for red herrings. If your institution has no distribution requirements outside the major, for instance, or requires daily church attendance, it clearly differs from most colleges. Both features call for some explanation, because many readers may perceive them as controversial. So unless your proposal is focused on curriculum reform or additional training in advising for faculty, you might omit a reference to distribution requirements from the general descriptive material. Required daily chapel demonstrates your institution's religious affiliation, but in this general section a statement of affiliation with the church is probably sufficient.

Is your institution located on 400 rolling acres on the shores of beautiful Lake Muddy Waters, 35 minutes from the center of the thriving metropolis of Bigtown? Subtract the adjectives; you're not writing a travel brochure or an admissions viewbook. Decide whether location is a factor. It may be, if Bigbucks Foundation or Worldwide Computer is in Bigtown, or if you're looking for funds to study water pollution or hoping to expand your student intern program. But if you're writing to a national organization about a project that doesn't depend on geography, don't waste the reader's time by mentioning it.

Recycling proposals

When you're raising money for a major project, you're often approaching a number of foundations and corporations. Inevitably, you'll use much of the same material. But it's crucial to edit each version of the proposal to make it appropriate for the specific organization to which you are sending it. Eliminate unnecessary information; add details that will strengthen the appeal of your project in this particular case. You may find that the proposal changes dramatically. What you send to Worldwide Computer, for instance, contains a broad and detailed description of the entire expansion of the curriculum and community-related activities. The Bigbucks Foundation, which is interested in art in the community, doesn't need anything nearly that elaborate. A two-paragraph description of the project provides the context for a detailed discussion of the gallery program.

Appendices

As you write a proposal you often find that the information you've accumulated would make your proposal about 50 pages long and discourage all but the most intrepid from reading it. Or the faculty in charge of the project have great qualifications but describing their training and subsequent professional activities would require several pages. Or you want to show that your institution is fiscally sound, and just saying so won't do it. The best way to add that material is to make it into attachments or appendices.

An appendix to your proposal should strengthen your case by backing up statements or assertions you've made in the proposal. It should provide information that is less central to your arguments, but is still important if the reader wants a broader picture of your institution. You should never put in an appendix the only reference to an important factor. For example, if you're writing a proposal about financial aid, you shouldn't confine to an appendix your only mention of the increased number of students receiving aid. But you could construct a graph or chart that would clearly and quickly convey the changes in the numbers of recipients and the aid budget so the reader doesn't have to wade through pages of descriptive material.

You can justify your claims in appendices. Your proposal for faculty development may say that your faculty members have strong records of professional activity, and you might cite several of their most notable recent publications. In an appendix you could list many more, choosing carefully to make sure that the publications (or exhibitions or performances) are really notable and not just fluff, and that many departments are represented. You would not, by the way, include copies of all those publications, although if an outside source, such as a newspaper or magazine, had published an article about the achievements of one or more of your faculty, you might include that as another appendix. An outside review, of whatever sort, conveys a certain degree of credibility. You can talk all you like about the increasing numbers of students who make Phi Beta Kappa, but your institution sets its own standards for membership in that honorary society. SAT scores or graduate school acceptances are more objective criteria in foundation and corporate eyes.

Charts and tables can be useful appendices. Rather than describing in the body of your proposal to Worldwide Computer how enrollments in foreign languages have grown year by year since 1980, you would put that data in table form. For the gallery proposal to the Bigbucks Foundation you could construct a table showing costs for the program each year, number of exhibitions, and number of ex-

Fact Sheet: Birnam Wood College

Founded: 1895, by members of the Wood family, as a men's college. Became coeducational in 1972.

Location: 50 miles east of Portland, in the scenic Dunsinane region. Main campus of 150 acres is surrounded by 17,000-acre forest preserve.

Degrees offered: B.A., B.S., M.S.

Facilities: Oak Science Center, built 1899, renovated 1975; Chestnut Hall (humanities and social sciences), built 1895; Hamm Drama Center, built 1971; "Dutch" Elm Hall (administration), built 1915; Spruce, Fir, Pine, Larch, and Magnolia (women only) Residence Halls; Forester Library (240,000 vols., 1,000 periodicals), built 1928, renovated 1972; Weyerhauser Student Center, built 1974; Willow Gymnasium, built 1964.

Enrollment: 1,484 (1,051 men, 433 women). 80 percent in top quadrant of high school class; 75 percent graduate in 4 years, 85 percent in 5 years. Minorities: 12.2 percent, including black, Hispanic, Asian, and foreign nationals. Geographic distribution: 36 states, 6 foreign countries.

Cost: Tuition, $8,825; room, board, and fees, $2,350. Financial aid awards need-based. Approximately 57 percent of all students receive some assistance from college sources.

Faculty: 135 FTE, 90 percent with Ph.D. or terminal degree.

Curriculum: 17 departments, 28 major fields plus special majors. 67 percent of students major in the sciences; 10 percent in fine arts/theater, and 23 percent in humanities.

Budget: $21,500,978 for 1984-85.

Endowment: $30,200,000 market value (6/1/84).

Constituent support: Alumni, $4,745,923 (31 percent participation); parents, $298,321; friends, $78,970; trustees, $421,899; corporations and foundations, $1,872,536 (6/1/83-5/31/84).

Governance: Board of trustees, Oakleigh Ashmore ('42), Chair; Macauley Duncan, Ph.D., President.

For further information: Office of the President, Birnam Wood College, Dunsinane, OR 80988, 809/367-7378

pected attendees. The purpose of those tables is to demonstrate that URC is a good place for the program to be established, so be careful that your charts don't contradict your prose. If you've said that interest in foreign languages has never been as strong as it is now, your figures should show increased enrollment, or you'd better have other convincing indicators.

Sometimes you may be well along in the proposal-writing stage before you discover, to your dismay, that what everyone has been telling you about increased enrollment in language courses has been based on a gut feeling rather than facts. Don't despair; there's almost certainly a reason for those gut feelings. Perhaps history faculty with special language skills have been getting a lot of requests for private tutorials, or students have been taking language courses at neighboring institutions. Did you ask for the right set of figures from the registrar's office? Go back to the folks who told you about all this interest in foreign languages and pin them down.

"There are lies, damned lies, and statistics," as the saying goes. Make sure your figures are honest. Compare enrollment of nonforeign minorities in 1975 with today's nonforeign minorities, not with all minority students, which might include students from other countries. If the educational and general budget has increased from $5 million to $10 million, it's doubled, or increased 100 percent, not 50 percent. Don't fudge, either deliberately or inadvertently. Check your numbers with those who supply them to you, and if you don't understand them, ask for more explanations. It's fairly safe to assume that if you don't know what a certain table is proving or what a .3 correlation indicates, your reader won't either. You may not need it or it may be the key datum on which your argument rests. But unless you understand it you'll never know.

Curriculum vitae (cv) is Latin for "the course of one's life," and indeed it is a summary of the professional life of a faculty member. What those of us in other professions call resumes are simple by comparison. You will often want to include a cv with a proposal, but don't be shy about asking the faculty member to shorten it. No one is going to read through three pages of titles of published articles and reviews. And you don't need to include the personal information (age, marital status, home address, and so forth). It's not relevant.

Be careful about supplying any sort of personal information in an appendix. When you are approaching a corporation you might want to include a list of graduates employed in the particular industry, but unless you have the permission of those named you're better off simply listing the companies that employ them. Once when I visited a member of a major accounting firm, I took with me a list of alumnae employed as accountants. He wanted a copy of that list; his firm was looking for women and minorities, and he wanted to do some raiding. Since I didn't have permission from any of the women on the list to give their names, I put him in touch with the career services office instead. And I didn't use that particular list as a proposal attachment.

Other specific information you might include as attachments could be copies of blueprints, if your project is bricks and mortar; a timetable or flow chart, if timing is a critical element of your project; the catalog of a recent art exhibit, in the case of a gallery request; an inventory of current computer hardware and a very specific description of the equipment for which you are requesting funds; the material distributed to all students applying to foreign programs and the list of criteria used by the faculty committee to decide eligibility; and so forth.

You can often present general information about your institution effectively in attachments. Standard enclosures might include a copy of the most recent auditors' report and a three-year budget to demonstrate financial stability; a list of current members of the board of trustees, so that the reader can see that your institution is well-connected; a copy of your institution's Letter of Determination from the Internal Revenue Service, which shows that your institution is a tax-exempt organization and thus eligible to receive grants; and a list of recent grants. The latter may change for each proposal. If you're approaching a local corporation or foundation you'll want to stress local support at any level, while a national foundation won't be impressed by $1,000 from your neighborhood manufacturing concern and will see its inclusion as an attempt to pad.

Another attachment of a general nature is a fact sheet (see the sample on page 58). This one-page description of your institution is a useful document for several purposes. You'll need a fact sheet when you are dealing with an organization with which your institution has no longstanding relationship, and those acting on your proposal need general information (enrollment, budget, library holdings, number of major fields, faculty-student ratio). The fact sheet provides all this in readily accessible form. No one has to flip through pages to discover that you offer the Ph.D. or that your physical plant was worth $92 million last year. I sometimes enclose a fact sheet when I write to ask for an appointment at a foundation or corporation with which my institution has no history. It's a quick way of establishing institutional credentials.

Don't include a college catalog unless it's requested. (You can always cut and copy the section that describes a particular department's program and lists its courses.) If you must include a glossy publication because it contains specific information, label it with the page number(s) so that the reader can turn immediately to the items of interest. If he or she keeps reading, so much the better, but don't make the reader work for the information. There are too many other demands on his or her time.

Preparing the finished copy

If you have access to a word processor, you have the luxury of testing your proposal's layout before preparing the final copy. Run off a draft with the headings you intend to use, in single or double space, just as you intend it to go out. You want it to look good on the page. This doesn't mean "think white space," as our colleagues in publications might say. You are relying on words to convince, and words—not pictures or colors—must be the focus of this document. But you want to make the document inviting to the reader. Don't pack your pages so full that the eye can't take them in; use standard size paper, with good margins at top and bottom, as well as at the sides. The basic 8½ x 11 paper has become a standard because, when you use proper margins, the eye can scan a line with ease. Don't use script or anything that looks "special," and do use a black ribbon. You don't want to distract the reader with gimmicks.

When word processing first became popular, many people took advantage of the mechanical ability to make the right-hand margin as regular as the left. Unfortunately, this "right justification" looked poor. Even the best printers had trouble producing spacing that made sentences easy to read, and the technique tended to results in proposals that looked mass-produced. Printers have improved, but the objections still stand. You don't have to go as far as the people at one institution, who believe in the mystique of the hand-typed proposal and won't send out anything that has been generated on the computer (although they have excellent equipment). But you do want the reader to be aware on many levels that the proposal is designed with his or her interest in mind, and right justification contradicts that impression.

Do use:

- headings,
- indentations of quotes or lists, and
- carets (sometimes known as bullets)

if they will make the proposal more comprehensible to the reader. You may want to set off some sections with narrower margins, just as you would set off a long quotation in a research paper. Sometimes making a list is effective. Be discreet, though, or you may find your proposal beginning to look like a direct mail piece.

If your proposal is long, supply a table of contents. This allows the reader to turn quickly to any particular section of the proposal. (But be sure your page references are correct after the inevitable last-minute revisions.) Number your pages, of course, but also supply page headings that give the date and the name of your institution, at a minimum. That's your protection against the proverbial gust of wind that scatters everything on the foundation staff member's desk.

A formal proposal is almost always typed double space, or at one and a half spacing, out of concern for the reader's comfort. He or she needs to be able to concentrate on your argument rather than on the mechanics of its presentation, and page after page of single-spaced typing can intimidate, bore, or actively repel the person you most want to persuade. Use pica type; it will make your proposal easy to read. The smaller the type, the harder it looks to read. A development officer recently told me of the special proposal his institution prepared for an elderly woman who controls substantial foundation assets. Because she has great difficulty seeing standard type, the proposal was typed on standard 8½ x 11 paper but with extremely wide margins; it was then photocopied on a machine that can enlarge the original. What emerged was a "large-type" proposal, which the recipient could read with no difficulty.

Check hyphenation. Word-processing programs almost all have options that allow you to hyphenate despite "word wrap," the function that removes the necessity of using the return key to end a line. Experienced secretaries can hyphenate without giving it a lot of thought, just as they can judge layout. But you still need to proofread carefully, especially if the proposal has been revised substantially. Read for sense and for mechanical errors. And check numbers. Did you change the amount requested to reflect the addition of the new position in sociology? And did you remember to change it in the summary paragraph at the end of the proposal as well as in the cover letter from the president?

Should you put the proposal and attachments in some sort of binder? Many are available; they range from simple manila folders with your institution's seal to ornate, spiral-bound or spring-closed covers. Your guiding principle is, as always, the convenience of the reader. If you need to keep a lot of material together—a two-page cover letter, 14 pages of formal proposal, 10 pages of appendices, a financial report, and some blueprints—you may want to put them in a folder of some sort. But keep it as simple as possible. Glitzy, expensive-looking folders won't help "sell your product"; they're more likely to raise questions about how much your institution really needs more money. And in many organizations the person who opens the mail will rip your proposal out of its folder, staple it together, and slap a routing slip on it.

How to deliver proposals is often a subject for debate. Is it impressive to use one of the express mail services, or does that convey a sense of last-minute haste and poor organization? Should the president or another high-ranking official hand-deliver the proposal and, if so, should this person have an appointment or just drop in, envelope in hand? How much trust can you put in the U.S. Postal Service? What if you mail the proposal in time but it doesn't arrive by the deadline? Much of the concern about deadlines springs from federal agency regulations, most of which require adherence to very specific deadlines and spell out procedures for validating delivery. Some foundations and corporations have guidelines for acceptance of proposals that come close to the federal ones. If that's the case, you must meet the deadline however you can. It won't matter how your proposal gets there as long as it arrives on time.

Use whatever delivery service is most convenient for you. One of the advantages of private delivery, whether by hand or by courier service, is that you know the proposal has arrived. But if you mail the proposal "return receipt requested," you can have that reassurance, too. Courier services usually deliver to the receptionist or secretary, so it's unlikely that you'll impress the staff with your worldliness or with your lack of timing. Hand delivery probably doesn't add much, one way or another, to your proposal's chances. By the time you've reached the proposal stage, the relationship is either well enough established so that another visit is unnecessary or so tenuous that one visit won't help. And dropping in may offend the staff member. You're assuming, after all, that this very busy person has nothing better to do than be interrupted by an unscheduled visit.

Once the proposal has been delivered safely and on time, you can begin follow-up procedures.

Chapter 5

Follow-up: What to Do After the Proposal Is in the Mail

By the time the document over which you have labored for so long is actually in the mail or on the Federal Express truck, you're probably so tired of the subject that you want to forget it completely and move on to something else. But you'll be doing your proposal, and your institution, a major disservice if you assume there's nothing more you can do about getting that grant. And you need to do a little housekeeping to be ready for the next proposal.

First, make sure a complete copy of the proposal, as it went out, is in the files. You may decide not to include a copy of the auditors' report or the college catalog, if those weighty documents were appended, and obviously you're not going to fill up your file drawers with copies of faculty publications. But at least include a list of every attachment, and it's not a bad idea to photocopy the express mail receipt. One purpose of this record-keeping is so that you'll be able to go back to the proposal when you're writing on a similar topic in the future. You may recycle some of the prose or use an appendix that lists graduates who have earned a Ph.D. in the humanities. It's perfectly legitimate to reuse parts of old proposals, although you have to be careful to focus the prose on the new recipient and to make sure that your statistics are up-to-date.

A complete copy serves another purpose as well. You might get a call from the president's office or, worse still, a curt note from the president attached to a copy of a letter: The foundation or corporation has received your proposal but must have a copy of your institution's tax-exempt letter, or catalog, or list of recent grants, before the proposal can be processed. You know you included that particular document with the proposal, and your file copy proves it. Be careful. Though it's nice to know that you did things correctly, don't use this fact as ammunition to argue with the president's office or, worse yet, with the foundation or corporation. Simply send another copy of the "missing" document. And use this opportunity to begin developing a relationship with the staff member who signed the letter or made the call. You may want to get back to this person later to determine the status of your proposal.

While you're making copies of the proposal, make enough for everyone on campus who should have one. This might include the president, the provost, and the faculty member who will be project director if the project is funded. They're the ones who will get calls from the foundation or corporation staff person who has questions about the proposal. If they have the actual document, they can provide answers without having to send to your office for a copy.

Some people just need a memo that acknowledges their contributions and tells them what to expect—"It's gone out...thanks for all your help. Keep your fingers crossed. We should hear something in six weeks." Your business manager will be much happier with advance knowledge of a project that will require some detailed bookkeeping, and the financial aid officer may want to be aware of the possibility of other income when he or she is looking at grant aid for next semester.

Sometimes you'll want to send a copy of the proposal to your outside helpers. If your proposal refers to the president of the local branch of the corporation, who can speak to the way your continuing education courses have helped his middle managers, you'd better be sure he has a copy. (And I assume you got his approval to mention his name in the proposal.) If your trustee has agreed to drop a note to her old friend, the executive director of a local foundation, send her a copy right away. It gives her the background she needs and also reminds her that it's time to follow through on what she agreed to do.

Some off-campus people don't need copies of the proposal; they just need to know that you've sent one and what it's for. In the case of a major request, the chair of the board of trustees, and perhaps all members of the trustee committee most involved in fund raising, should know what's happening. People in power tend to travel in the same circles, and some of your board members may know some of the members of the corporate or foundation board who will be considering your proposal. If your board members know about the proposal, they can put in a good word when the opportunity arises. At the very least, they won't have the embarrassment of appearing uninformed when they run into their corporate or foundation colleagues at the museum benefit or the symphony or the neighborhood Christmas party.

Even after you've sent the request, you need to maintain other sorts of contact with staff at the foundation or corporation. You want them to pay attention to your proposal. The first sign of this may be a postcard or letter that tells you the proposal has arrived; because this takes time and money, only a few organizations do it. It's always a relief to get that notification, but you don't have to wait for the organization to contact you. I think it's perfectly appropriate to call the foundation or corporation after two weeks to make sure that your proposal has arrived. Be prepared to talk to someone who doesn't know, though; it may take time for a staff member to track down your request.

Calling to arrange an appointment for someone from your institution to talk to a foundation or corporate staff member is a slightly stronger move. You can set up that possibility in the proposal or the cover letter. But be sure that if your president or project director offers to "call within the next few weeks to arrange a site visit," he or she follows through. Put a note on your call-up calendar. You may have to hang around and bug the president till the call is actually made, but do it. A visit to your campus provides a wonderful chance to give someone from the grant-making organization a firsthand glimpse of why your request should be funded. If the staff members are so busy that they can't make time for a site visit or if policy precludes one, at least you've been in contact with the foundation or corporation and given their people another reason to recognize, and look favorably on, your institution.

Keep in touch in other ways. Have you received other funds for the project? Gotten the blueprints from the architect? Enrolled the largest class in a decade? Hired a Nobel prize-winner? Balanced the budget for the fourteenth consecutive year? Send a letter and a copy of the audited figures "to update the financial information that accompanied our proposal."

Some proposals seem to disappear into the void. Despite your efforts to be sure the people at the corporation or foundation know all the right things about your institution, you still hear nothing. But there are steps you can take, even then; you don't have to sit and wait for the phone to ring or the postman to knock. If you had an outside helper, a trustee or friend who spoke for you, ask that person to inquire directly or indirectly. Often, though, the volunteer will feel uncomfortable about doing this and it will be up to you to make the contact.

Do you know when the corporate or foundation board will meet? If so, you can call and ask what the decision was. That's a frightening idea, I know. No one likes to be rejected, and somehow the telephone, because of its immediacy, makes us feel vulnerable. What if it's bad news? But there are times when it's important to know where your institution stands—if, for instance, you have a number of requests for the same project pending with different organizations and you need to know just how much money you can expect. Perhaps you'd like to submit a proposal about the same project to a different corporation, if this one isn't going to give you the money, and the second organization's deadline is approaching. Or your board is about to meet and is anxious about the status of the proposal. You're not out of line to call the foundation or corporation about your request. Many foundations and corporations have a policy of notifying everyone at the same time, in writing, and preparing the letters after a board meeting can take time. Staffers will almost always tell you the good—or bad—news. Frankly, the most frustrating news is that they've delayed consideration of your request until the next meeting. Then you've got to repeat all the same actions.

When you finally hear from the foundation or corporation, there are several things you *must* do immediately, whether you got the grant or your request was denied. First, make sure that the president's office hears the news. Sometimes that's where you got the word, because notification went directly to the top. But unless the president tells you about the grant, it's a good idea to send something in writing to his or her attention. Travel schedules, vast amounts of mail, and understandable human error can prevent a president from getting messages. One of your jobs is to make sure that you've done everything you can to keep the president informed about the status of the proposal.

Next, notify those involved with the project: the project director, the appropriate dean, the chair of the department, the trustee or alumna who reinforced your efforts. Then acknowledge the organization's communication. A turndown deserves a thank-you note just as much as a grant does. Take the long view; you and your colleagues may be distressed that your wonderful project was rejected, and you may be depressed about long-range chances for support, but those feelings are temporary. Sure as the start of the next semester, someone will need money for a project that seems to fit beautifully with what the Bigbucks Foundation is doing now. And you'll be in much better shape to reopen negotiations with the Bigbucks staff if your president sent a gracious, regretful note than if nothing was said or, worse yet, someone tried to argue with the foundation's decision.

In the happy event that the foundation or corporation has agreed to make the grant, there are a number of additional steps to take. Talk with the principals—the project director, the dean, the financial aid person, whoever will be in charge of spending the money—and make sure they know what's expected. Lag time between when you submitted the proposal and when you get the grant can be so great that people forget what they agreed to do. This is especially true of faculty who, in many cases, are committing themselves some 18 months in advance. Supply fresh copies of the proposal and of the written notification from the grant-making organization. If any provisions are unclear, offer to call the foundation or corporation staff person for an explanation. Offer to remind the project director well before the deadlines when reports must be sent to the grant-making organization, and keep extra copies of the reporting forms, if the organization supplies them. Note deadlines for your own calendar so that you can make sure reports have been filed or prepare drafts for the president, if the reports should come from that office.

If a condition of the grant is that your institution will set up a special lecture series, name scholars, or establish an endowment, or the board of trustees has to vote to accept any endowed fund, make sure that those processes are underway. Your responsibility for overseeing the implementation of the grant will vary according to the type of institution you work at and your own level of responsibility. In a large office you may do nothing; writing the proposal was your only responsibility. In a small shop you may be in charge of finding the special lecturers and arranging a dinner party for major donors when the key speaker will be on campus. Whatever your tasks, though, the more you are aware of the impact of a grant—not just what it does for the faculty or students, but the other ways it can affect your institution—the better you will be able to write other proposals. You'll remember, and be able to reflect in prose, those less obvious benefits.

You may need to talk to the people in the business office and make sure they have a copy of the proposal or at least the budget. If the granting agency has made any changes in the amounts you requested and the purposes for which you requested them, the people at your institution who are going to be handling the money should be aware of them. (The people who will be spending the money should be aware of them, too.) Staff in the business office should be aware of reporting requirements, since preparation of expenditure reports may be their responsibility. In most cases, whether responsibility for those reports technically falls to the business people or to the faculty, the business office will put a considerable amount of time into their preparation. Relations between faculty members and business office staff are notoriously poor, and one of the most helpful things you can do (*if* you can do it) is to get the project directors and the appropriate business staff members to sit down together at the beginning of the project. Each "side" can then explain its requirements and schedules and can begin to understand how the other half functions. This won't prevent problems, but it may ease communications.

Your institution will certainly want to take advantage of any ways the grant could generate publicity. In the small shop, you may be the best person to explain the grant to the public relations people. (In some cases, you may *be* the PR person.) Depending on your institution, the nature of the request being funded, the amount of funds, and the status of the donor, the PR people could notify the *New York Times,* CBS, your local weekly, the alumni magazine, the student newspaper, and the *Chronicle of Higher Education.* Your responsibilities include making sure that what the PR people write is accurate, and that any releases have been cleared with the foundation or corporation that made the grant. Some agencies, such as the Andrew W. Mellon Foundation and the William and Flora Hewlett Foundation, make it a condition of the grant that you clear any release with their staff. Others say they merely want copies of what appears in print. Whatever they say, it never hurts to contact the organization before a release is issued to let someone know what's happening. It's a courtesy, perhaps, but an important one; just as you would clear releases with the president's office, so that he or she is aware of what's being said about your institution, you need to be certain that the other side of the transaction—the donor—is agreeable to appearing in the media.

Once the project is underway and the incumbent is selected for the chair or the scholarship recipients are named, share this news with the grant-making organization. People like to know that their money is being put to good use, and when it's not their own money, it's important to keep reassuring them that they made a good decision on how to spend it. Fight the tendency to consider the grant-making process complete when the check is in hand; part of your job is stewardship. Saying thank you for current support also paves the way for future requests.

Use an event connected with the grant as a means of getting a key representative of the foundation or corporation to campus. If a corporation has given you a grant for economics, invite the president and board chair to hear John Kenneth Galbraith speak, or suggest that those sending out the special invitations include the VIPs from "your" grantors. Be aware of what's happening on campus. You may not be planning to attend the lecture or the gallery opening, but be alert to ways of involving donors or potential donors. Involve faculty and students with people from the foundation or corporation, too. They are the reason your institution exists, and they're its best advertisement.

Even if the grant maker doesn't request formal reports, keep in touch. Many presidents send anniversary letters, or some sort of yearly letter, to corporate and foundation supporters and even to some that do not currently support the institution. This is a good opportunity to inform the organization about what's been happening on campus in general and, more specifically, in the areas of greatest interest to the grant maker. Sometimes, in cases where a corporation or foundation makes annual unrestricted grants, this letter becomes the proposal. The message is basically, "We've had a great year, thanks in part to your support; won't you help us again?" Unfortunately, increased competition for corporate and foundation dollars has decreased the number of agencies that will respond to this.

If you are drafting a more detailed report for the donor, you'll repeat a good deal of the proposal-writing process: gathering and organizing information, writing and rewriting in an appropriate format, checking data (and drafts) with the principals to make sure you've accurately reflected what's been accomplished—and what hasn't. Be honest. If the project was well thought out in the first place, and those involved with it are qualified to do what they said they wanted to do, and yet there are problems, there are almost always good reasons for those problems. Perhaps it simply took longer to develop software than anyone expected. Or perhaps unemployment in Spain climbed sharply, and the companies that promised you 50 internships could only supply 25. The people receiving your report will understand and accept explanations of difficulties; what they won't like is receiving a report that tells them everything is wonderful and discovering later that things are not wonderful at all. *That* will really destroy your institution's credibility.

On the other hand, a good report can give your institution a major boost towards the funding of its next request. The organization will know about your institution. They may have met some of your faculty and students, and they will surely have been impressed with the businesslike way the project was handled. You, too, will find it easier to put together another request, because there will be some faces (or at least voices) to attach to names, and you'll probably understand in considerably greater depth what the foundation or corporation really wants to accomplish with its philanthropy.

But what do you do if your proposal is rejected? After you've taken the steps described earlier—notification of those involved and acknowledgement of the organization's letter—you go back to the drawing board. Find out why. You'll have to work at it. Unlike government agencies, foundations and corporations are under no legal obligation to share the reasons for their decisions with you. While many are willing to do so, demands on staff time are enormous, and it's more productive to spend time overseeing activities of recipients and screening new applications than providing each unsuccessful applicant with detailed reasons for the rejection.

How do you get this information? The telephone is the most effective instrument. A visit is great if the staff member has time to see you, because you can use it to lay the groundwork for another approach, but you'll often find that staff members don't want to see disappointed applicants for a while. And it's unusual to find a staff member willing to put in writing the reasons for turning you down. Time is a factor; so, too, is a desire to avoid liability. It's safer not to put anything on paper except the most general comments. So use the telephone. And remember that you're asking for information and advice. Even though the foundation or corporation turned you down, the staff member (and indeed the organization) is not an adversary. Your ego may be smarting, but it's crucial to remain dispassionate.

And, in fact, few proposals are declined because of the way they're written. In many cases, you'll find that your proposal was declined not because of any fault in its preparation, or because your institution is unworthy of support, but because the foundation or corporation has limited resources and simply can't fund all the good causes that come its way. A rejection letter often says this, and it's one of the hardest objections to overcome. What the organization often means is, "We don't know you as well as we know some other applicants." Conversation with a staff member will elicit the fact that an institution similar to yours gets grants regularly because of a recruiting relationship or overlapping board membership or a project that fits precisely with the donor organization's objectives. You haven't done anything wrong; some other institutions simply have better relationships with this particular organization.

If this is the message, ask for advice: What should we do to improve our relationship? And if you're told that you should cultivate the acquaintance of top corporate people, and that inviting the chair of the company's board to speak at your institution may help, make sure the people on campus know this. They may not invite him, but at least everyone knows there's no point in knocking on the door of that organization until there's a change of personnel at the top of the company— or of your institution.

If the objection is programmatic—the foundation staff didn't think that the project your School of Education has designed for in-service training of math and science teachers will be effective—don't argue. Try to get as much specific information as possible. Was it the classroom component? The fact that you'd be relying on teaching materials produced five years ago? Was there some feeling that the project director hadn't had enough experience to manage a program of this magnitude? Relay staff comments to those involved in designing the program (and make sure you've put them in writing for your files). You may have set the stage for a dialog between the School of Education and the foundation that could lead to another, successful proposal.

Keep in touch with the foundation or corporation. Send your annual report, literary magazine, or whatever publication your institution produces that fits most closely with the organization's interests. Try to visit, at least annually, unless the door was firmly closed in your face. (And this happens; I've dealt with several foundations and corporations who have said bluntly, "Don't call us, we'll call you.") If your project was declined but the relationship is cordial, you may want to send the organization occasional progress reports. Don't gloat, but let them know that in spite of their decision your institution is accomplishing great things. In short, keep cultivating them.

And keep an eye on them from a distance. Watch for news of their grant-making activity and for changes in staff or leadership. Talk with your peers, especially those whose institutions succeeded in getting grants. Be aware of deadlines. If you can submit a proposal only once in a calendar year, put a note to yourself on your call-up calendar two months before that anniversary so you can reexamine the situation and decide whether to try again. And don't be discouraged; next year you may succeed.

Chapter 6

Tools of the Trade

Take advantage of whatever labor-saving devices you can and press for more. Your job is to write proposals. Whether you're the whole office, typing the finished version as well as doing the research and writing, or whether you have a staff of 15 reporting to you, the less time you must spend on the mechanics of proposal preparation the more time you have to write. Measured against the cost of additional staff, none of the equipment described below is expensive, and even if your operation is very small, those in charge should see the wisdom of investing in it. You may be able to share some of it with other departments, too.

The dictaphone

You may be able to type 100 words per minute or have a lifelong addiction to drafting on yellow legal paper, but you owe it to yourself to learn how to use a dictaphone. It saves time and it's portable. Almost all of us can speak faster than we can type, and our time is better spent collecting information, analyzing what we've collected, and drafting numerous documents (not just proposals, but memos to file, letters, and reports) than typing or writing in longhand.

Even if you're the one who does the typing, use the dictaphone. Use it in the office and take it with you wherever you go. Treat it like a diary; make notes or lists of tasks to be done. Debrief as you drive from one appointment to the next, while the details of who said what and what needs to be done are fresh in your mind. I've sat in airports and railroad stations, on park benches, in corners of hotel lobbies, and in reception areas at major corporations and talked into my dictaphone. Sometimes people stare, but does that matter?

With practice you can learn to dictate first drafts of proposals. Rely on your outline to keep you on track. One of the advantages of dictating is that it makes you

WRITING WINNING PROPOSALS

pay attention to the way things sound. People do "hear" as they read, and you'll become conscious of the need for some rhythm and variety of sentence structure as you listen to what you're dictating.

You may find the dictaphone inhibiting at first; many people aren't accustomed to hearing themselves speak. I persuaded myself very early that I wasn't talking to a machine but either to my secretary, who would be typing from the tape, or to the person to whom I was writing the letter. I sometimes have to revise what I've dictated because it's become a little too informal in tone—it reads like speech, rather than writing—but I think my letters, on the whole, benefit from the way the machine lets me speak directly to the reader.

Another hurdle can be punctuation. Some secretaries can punctuate by sound; they can hear that you are beginning a new sentence and are familiar enough with rules of punctuation to know when a comma is needed. But such people are rare, and you'll probably have to dictate the punctuation, too. Prepare yourself, as well, to spell proper names and technical terms the first time you use them. You'll be surprised at how easy it is to indicate new paragraphs, semicolons, lists, or spelling; once you've gotten used to the machine, you'll find that these "mechanical" insertions don't break your flow of thought.

You can purchase a dictaphone for as little as $50 or as much as several hundred dollars. I have inherited the ones I've used. If you have the opportunity to buy a new one, try several. Test the various buttons and switches for convenience, ease of use, and size in relation to the size of your hand. Test the pickup: Do you want a unit that you must hold close to your mouth or one that will pick up speech from arm's length? (The latter may also pick up a lot of background noise.) What size tapes does it require? What size batteries and how many? Are they easy to get?

You'll also need a transcribing unit, which generally consists of a tape-playing machine, earphones, and some sort of device (usually a pedal) to make the tape play. These cost anywhere from $100 to $1,000. You'll need tapes, too. Don't economize here; you'll use them over and over. Have more than you think you'll need. If you take your dictaphone on business trips, which I certainly advise you to do, you can mail or express tapes back to your office so that transcriptions will be ready when you return.

I have seen but not used a special kind of recorder that works with a telephone answering device. You can dictate up to 15 minutes, call the phone to which the device is attached, and trigger a rapid-play system that allows the answering device to record from your dictaphone in less than a minute. You can retrieve messages the same way and then play back your tape at regular speed to hear your messages.

The computer

Is there anyone who isn't convinced of the wonders of computer-based word processing? For those of us who've been writing proposals for a decade or more, the change from typewriters to computers has been especially dramatic and welcome. Gone are the days of correction fluid (in several colors if you used color-coded carbons). Even the self-correcting typewriter is a thing of the past. We don't fear revision nearly as much as we used to, nor do we dread that final proofreading that always turns up a typo in the middle of the second page. We writers tend to be picky souls, and the computer lets us revise to our hearts' content—or at least until the deadline approaches.

You should be using a computer for word processing. I'd say that every organization in this country sophisticated enough to know about applying for grants has access, somehow, to a computer. Many local libraries make them available for patrons. Apple Computer has donated hundreds to community organizations. Even if you volunteer your time and your entire organization is run by volunteers on a shoestring, someone in the organization has a computer at home or at his or her office. Find out what kind it is; borrow appropriate word-processing software and draft your proposal on it.

The cost of personal computers has declined dramatically over the past few years and will undoubtedly decline even further. The personal computer (PC) I bought in November 1983 now sells for one-third less than I paid (with a substantial discount). For half of what I paid for that machine, I can buy one with twice the capacity and infinitely more software available to it. Even if you don't have a PC at home, an institution that can pay you to write proposals should have at least one computer that you can use.

If you don't know how to use the computer, learn. I'm not suggesting that you become your own secretary, although many of us function in that capacity from time to time, but if you know how to find, edit, and print a document you may be able to head off an emergency. As I said earlier, doing your own typing is not the best use of your (expensive) time. But you should know how to use a computer because the technology is part of modern life, and because the students at your institution are becoming familiar with it. To get a complete picture of your institution, you need to understand this aspect of modern education, whether the curriculum includes courses in programming, machine language, electronic engineering, or merely computer-assisted learning modules.

The computer is infinitely more powerful than a typewriter, and you may find that you want to explore some applications beyond simple word processing. There is software that lets you check spelling, for instance. This can be helpful if you don't rely on it completely. The computer will compare every word of your proposal to the "dictionary" contained in its memory and will identify those words that don't match the dictionary spellings. The pitfalls here are several: You're limited to the words in the dictionary, and proper names and technical terms are generally not included, although some dictionaries are designed so you can add to them, temporarily or permanently. The spelling checker checks only spelling. It won't pick up misused words, grammatical errors, omitted lines, or incorrect punctuation. It is very good for typos of common words: "teh" for "the," "adn" for "and," "bu" instead of "but." However, it's no substitute for careful proofreading. It won't see "an" as a typo for "and."

Some programs offer frequency checkers. With this option you can find out how many times you've used "undergraduate," "however," or "at this point in time" (which, I hope, is never). It can even tell you how many semicolons you've used. Many word-processing programs have "search" options, which can be used in much the same way. With the cursor at the top of your document, you can order the computer to look for all the places where you've used the word "institution"; your proposal then scrolls until the word is found and remains there while you decide whether to leave it or replace it.

I haven't used spread sheets very much yet, so my recommendations are based on reports from more experienced colleagues. On the whole, ratings are favorable, although most spread sheets are not particularly user-friendly and require mastery of a fairly complex series of commands as well as the ability to write mathematical formulas. However, once you've acquired the knowledge to use programs such as Lotus 1-2-3 or VisiCalc, you can produce budgets and know they balance, and you can make changes with very little effort.

For example, if you're preparing that enormous costs and funding report for URC's curriculum revision (see *Budget 1*, p. 33), and the provost tells you that the language department will add one full-time person (with benefits) and two part-timers, rather than two full-time and one part-time, you can make changes in the salary column and (if you've put in the correct formulas) expect the changes to be reflected in the benefits and totals columns as well. The problem here is that you need skill with formulas. Also, you must remember that changes in the budget don't automatically appear in the proposal.

There are lots of data base management programs, and I've worked with two: DBase III and a custom-designed model for Lake Forest College's Digital Equipment Company PDP 11/44. The program on the central system is enormous and quite flexible, from what I hear of other central systems; it is also full to overflowing. Learning to manipulate it was fun and taught me a great deal about machine logic. It let me collect a good deal of information about many corporations and foundations and then sort it by almost 100 fields of interest: location, name, previous support (by year and by account), funding interests, proposal deadlines and status, and so forth. However, DBase III enables me to do the same thing on a microcomputer and design custom forms as well.

If you have a microcomputer and no central computerized record system, you should probably try to develop your own data base. It's very useful to be able to generate a list of corporate and foundation prospects in the New York City area without having to rely on paper files or your own memory. It's also helpful to keep up-to-date records of the status of proposals: what's pending, being drafted, undergoing revision, needed. You can use the computer as a calendar and put items on call-up: ABC Foundation needs a presidential visit in March; when the board approves the auditors' report, send it to all the corporations where you have proposals pending, and so on.

As to what kind of computer system or microcomputer or software to get, there are many different machines and packages. You'll have to look them over, try them out, and make your own decision. My only suggestion is to go ahead and get something, anything, rather than trying to do a thorough survey and find the "best" system for you. Especially if you've never used a computer or a particular type of software, it's very difficult to decide what makes one better than another. Trying to figure out your needs when you've never used a computer and don't know what it can do for you is like trying to look up a word in the dictionary before you've learned to read. Sometimes it makes sense to get what your colleagues have so you can ask them for help; many of us find we can't learn by reading the directions, but have to experiment and call for help when we get stuck.

Building a library

Having research materials close to hand can save you a great deal of time. If your organization's resources don't permit you to assemble a large collection, however, you can always use the local library and the cooperating collections of the Foundation Center (see page 76). If the budget will stretch that far, you might join the Associates' program of the Foundation Center. The bibliography that follows is by no means conclusive; more materials are being produced all the time. You may find that you're more comfortable with some source books than others. Unless your budget is unlimited, you'll want to pick and choose according to your organization's particular needs.

THE FOUNDATION CENTER NETWORK

The Foundation Center is an independent national service organization established by foundations to provide an authoritative source of information on private philanthropic giving. In fulfilling its mission, The Center disseminates information on private giving through public service programs, publications and through a national network of library reference collections for free public use. The New York, Washington, DC, Cleveland and San Francisco reference collections operated by The Foundation Center offer a wide variety of services and comprehensive collections of information on foundations and grants. The Cooperating Collections are libraries, community foundations and other nonprofit agencies that provide a core collection of Foundation Center publications and a variety of supplementary materials and services in subject areas useful to grantseekers.

Over 100 of the network members have sets of private foundation information returns (IRS Form 990PF) for their states or regions which are available for public use. These collections are indicated by a • next to their names. A complete set of U.S. foundation returns can be found at the New York and Washington, DC collections. The Cleveland and San Francisco offices contain IRS returns for those foundations in the midwestern and western states respectively.

Because the collections vary in their hours, materials and services, **IT IS RECOMMENDED THAT YOU CALL EACH COLLECTION IN ADVANCE.**

To check on new locations or current information, call toll-free 1 800 424-9836.

REFERENCE COLLECTIONS OPERATED BY
THE FOUNDATION CENTER

• The Foundation Center
79 Fifth Avenue
New York, New York 10003
212-620-4230

• The Foundation Center
1001 Connecticut Avenue, NW
Washington, D.C. 20036
202-331-1400

• The Foundation Center
Kent H. Smith Library
1442 Hanna Building
1422 Euclid Avenue
Cleveland, Ohio 44115
216-861-1933

• The Foundation Center
312 Sutter Street
San Francisco, California
94108
415-397-0902

COOPERATING COLLECTIONS

Those collections marked with a bullet (•) have sets of private foundation information returns (IRS Form 990-PF) for their states or regions, available for public reference.

ALABAMA

• Birmingham Public Library
2020 Park Place
Birmingham 35203
205-226-3600

Huntsville–Madison County Public Library
108 Fountain Circle
P.O. Box 443
Huntsville 35804
205-536-0021

• Auburn University at Montgomery Library
Montgomery 36193 - 0401
205-271-9649

ALASKA

• University of Alaska,
Anchorage Library
3211 Providence Drive
Anchorage 99504
907-786-1848

ARIZONA

• Phoenix Public Library
Business and Sciences Department
12 East McDowell Road
Phoenix 85004
602-262-4782

• Tucson Public Library
Main Library
200 South Sixth Avenue
Tucson 85701
607-791-4393

ARKANSAS

• Westark Community College Library
Grand Avenue at Waldron Road
Fort Smith 72913
501-785-4241

• Little Rock Public Library
Reference Department
700 Louisiana Street
Little Rock 72201
501-370-5950

CALIFORNIA

Inyo County Library–
Bishop Branch
210 Academy Street
Bishop 93514
619-872-8091

• California Community Foundation
Funding Information Center
3580 Wilshire Blvd., Suite 1660
Los Angeles 90010
213-413-4042

• Community Foundation for
Monterey County
420 Pacific Street
Monterey 93940
408-375-9712

California Community Foundation
4050 Metropolitan Drive #300
Orange 92668
714-937-9077

Riverside Public Library
3581 7th Street
Riverside 92501
714-787-7201

California State Library
Reference Services, Rm. 309
914 Capital Mall
Sacramento 95814
916-322-4570

• San Diego Community Foundation
625 Broadway, Suite 1015
San Diego 92101
619-239-8815

• Orange County Community
Developmental Council
1440 East First Street, 4th Floor
Santa Ana 92701
714-547-6801

• Penisula Community Foundation
1204 Burlingame Avenue
Burlingame, 94011-0627
415-342-2505

• Santa Barbara Public Library
Reference Section
40 East Anapamu
P.O. Box 1019
Santa Barbara 931
805-962-7653

Santa Monica
1343 Sixth Str
Santa Monica
213-458-8603

Tuolomne County Library
465 S. Washington Street
Sonora 95370
209-533-5707

North Coast Opportunities, Inc.
101 West Church Street
Ukiah 95482
707-462-1954

COLORADO

Pikes Peak Library District
20 North Cascade Avenue
Colorado Springs 80901
303-473-2080

• Denver Public Library
Sociology Division
1357 Broadway
Denver 80203
303-571-2190

CONNECTICUT

Danbury Public Library
155 Deer Hill Avenue
Danbury 06810
203-797-4505

• Hartford Public Library
Reference Department
500 Main Street
Hartford 06103
203-525-9121

D.A.T.A.
880 Asylum Avenue
Hartford 06105
203-278-2477

D.A.T.A.
25 Science Park
Suite 502
New Haven 06513
203-786-5225

DELAWARE

• Hugh Morris Library
University of Delaware
Newark 19717-5267
302-451-2965

FLORIDA

Volusia County Public Library
City Island
Daytona Beach 32014
904-252-8374

- Jacksonville Public Library
Business, Science, and
    Industry Department
122 North Ocean Street
Jacksonville 32202
904-633-3926

- Miami–Dade Public Library
Florida Collection
One Biscayne Boulevard
Miami 33132
305-579-5001

- Orlando Public Library
10 North Rosalind
Orlando 32801
305-425-4694

- University of West Florida
John C. Pace Library
Pensacola 32514
904-474-2412

Selby Public Library
1001 Boulevard of the Arts
Sarasota 33577
813-366-7303

- Leon County Public Library
Community Funding
    Resources Center
1940 North Monroe Street
Tallahassee 32303
904-478-2665

Palm Beach County
    Community Foundation
324 Datura Street, Suite 311
West Palm Beach 33401
305-659-6800

GEORGIA

- Atlanta–Fulton Public Library
Ivan Allen Department
1 Margaret Mitchell Square
Atlanta 30303
404-688-4636

HAWAII

- Thomas Hale Hamilton Library
General Reference
University of Hawaii
2550 The Mall
Honolulu 96822
808-948-7214

Community Resource Center
The Hawaiian Foundation
Financial Plaza of the Pacific
111 South King Street
Honolulu 96813
808-525-8548

IDAHO

- Caldwell Public Library
1010 Dearborn Street
Caldwell 83605
208-459-3242

ILLINOIS

Belleville Public Library
121 East Washington Street
Belleville 62220
618-234-0441

DuPage Township
300 Briarcliff Road
Bolingbrook 60439
312-759-1317

- Donors Forum of Chicago
208 South LaSalle Street
Chicago 60604
312-726-4882

- Evanston Public Library
1703 Orrington Avenue
Evanston 60201
312-866-0305

- Sangamon State University
    Library
Shepherd Road
Springfield 62708
217-786-6633

INDIANA

Allen County Public Library
900 Webster Street
Fort Wayne 46802
219-424-7241

Indiana University Northwest
    Library
3400 Broadway
Gary 46408
219-980-6580

- Indianapolis–Marion County
    Public Library
40 East St. Clair Street
Indianapolis 46204
317-269-1733

IOWA

- Public Library of Des Moines
100 Locust Street
Des Moines 50308
515-283-4259

KANSAS

- Topeka Public Library
Adult Services Department
1515 West Tenth Street
Topeka 66604
913-233-2040

- Wichita Public Library
223 South Main
Wichita 67202
316-262-0611

KENTUCKY

Western Kentucky University
Division of Library Services
Helm-Cravens Library
Bowling Green 42101
502-745-3951

- Louisville Free Public Library
Fourth and York Streets
Louisville 40203
503-223-7201

LOUISIANA

- East Baton Rouge Parish Library
Centroplex Library
120 St. Louis Street
Baton Rouge 70821
504-389-4960

- New Orleans Public Library
Business and Science Division
219 Loyola Avenue
New Orleans 70140
504-596-2583

- Shreve Memorial Library
424 Texas Street
Shreveport 71101
318-226-5894

MAINE

- University of Southern Maine
Center for Research and
    Advanced Study
246 Deering Avenue
Portland 04102
207-780-4411

MARYLAND

- Enoch Pratt Free Library
Special Science and History
    Department
400 Cathedral Street
Baltimore 21201
301-396-5320

MASSACHUSETTS

- Associated Grantmakers of
    Massachusetts
294 Washington Street
Suite 501
Boston 02108
617-426-2608

- Boston Public Library
Copley Square
Boston 02117
617-536-5400

Walpole Public Library
Common Street
Walpole 02081
617-668-5497 ext. 340

Western Massachusetts Funding
    Resource Center
Campaign for Human Development
Chancery Annex
73 Chestnut Street
Springfield 01103
413-732-3175 ext. 67

- Grants Resource Center
Worcester Public Library
Salem Square
Worcester 01608
617-799-1655

MICHIGAN

- Alpena County Library
211 North First Avenue
Alpena 49707
517-356-6188

University of Michigan–Ann Arbor
Reference Department
209 Hatcher Graduate Library
Ann Arbor 48109-1205
313-764-1149

- Henry Ford Centennial Library
16301 Michigan Avenue
Dearborn 48126
313-943-2337

- Purdy Library
Wayne State University
Detroit 48202
313-577-4040

- Michigan State University Libraries
Reference Library
East Lansing 48824
517-353-9184

- Farmington Community Library
32737 West 12 Mile Road
Farmington Hills 48018
313-553-0300

- University of Michigan–Flint
    Library
Reference Department
Flint 48503
313-762-3408

- Grand Rapids Public Library
Sociology and Education Dept.
Library Plaza
Grand Rapids 49502
616-456-4411

- Michigan Technological
    University Library
Highway U.S. 41
Houghton 49931
906-487-2507

MINNESOTA

- Duluth Public Library
520 Superior Street
Duluth 55802
218-723-3802

- Southwest State University Library
Marshall 56258
507-537-7278

- Minneapolis Public Library
Sociology Department
300 Nicollet Mall
Minneapolis 55401
612-372-6555

Rochester Public Library
Broadway at First Street, SE
Rochester 55901
507-285-8002

Saint Paul Public Library
90 West Fourth Street
Saint Paul 55102
612-292-6311

MISSISSIPPI

Jackson Metropolitan Library
301 North State Street
Jackson 39201
601-944-1120

MISSOURI

- Clearinghouse for Midcontinent
    Foundations
Univ. of Missouri, Kansas City
Law School, Suite 1-300
52nd Street and Oak
Kansas City 64113
816-276-1176

- Kansas City Public Library
311 East 12th Street
Kansas City 64106
816-221-2685

- Metropolitan Association for
    Philanthropy, Inc.
5585 Pershing Avenue
Suite 150
St. Louis 63112
314-361-3900

- Springfield–Greene County
    Library
397 East Central Street
Springfield 65801
417-866-4636

MONTANA

- Eastern Montana College Library
Reference Department
1500 N. 30th Street
Billings 59101-0298
406-657-2262

- Montana State Library
Reference Department
1515 E. 6th Avenue
Helena 59620
406-444-3004

NEBRASKA

University of Nebraska, Lincoln
106 Love Library
Lincoln 68588-0410
402-472-2526

- W. Dale Clark Library
Social Sciences Department
215 South 15th Street
Omaha 68102
402-444-4826

NEVADA

• Las Vegas—Clark County
  Library District
  1401 East Flamingo Road
  Las Vegas 89109
  702-733-7810

• Washoe County Library
  301 South Center Street
  Reno 89505
  702-785-4190

NEW HAMPSHIRE

• The New Hampshire
  Charitable Fund
  One South Street
  Concord 03301
  603-225-6641

Littleton Public Library
109 Main Street
Littleton 03561
603-444-5741

NEW JERSEY

Cumberland County Library
800 E. Commerce Street
Bridgeton 08302
609-455-0080

The Support Center
17 Academy Street, Suite 1101
Newark 07102
201-643-5774

County College of Morris
Masten Learning Resource Center
Route 10 and Center Grove Road
Randolph 07869
201-361-5000 x470

• New Jersey State Library
  Governmental Reference
  185 West State Street
  Trenton 08625
  609-292-6220

NEW MEXICO

Albuquerque Community
  Foundation
6400 Uptown Boulevard N.E.
Suite 500-W
Albuquerque 87110
505-883-6240

• New Mexico State Library
  325 Don Gaspar Street
  Santa Fe 87503
  505-827-3824

NEW YORK

• New York State Library
  Cultural Education Center
  Humanities Section
  Empire State Plaza
  Albany 12230
  518-474-7645

Bronx Reference Center
New York Public Library
2556 Bainbridge Avenue
Bronx 10458
212-220-6575

Brooklyn in Touch
101 Willoughby Street
Room 1508
Brooklyn 11201
718-237-9300

• Buffalo and Erie County
  Public Library
  Lafayette Square
  Buffalo 14203
  716-856-7525

Huntington Public Library
338 Main Street
Huntington 11743
516-427-5165

• Levittown Public Library
  Reference Department
  One Bluegrass Lane
  Levittown 11756
  516-731-5728

SUNY/College at Old
  Westbury Library
223 Store Hill Road
Old Westbury 11568
516-876-3201

• Plattsburgh Public Library
  Reference Department
  15 Oak Street
  Plattsburgh 12901
  518-563-0921

Adriance Memorial Library
93 Market Street
Poughkeepsie 12601
914-485-4790

Queens Borough Public Library
89-11 Merrick Boulevard
Jamaica 11432
718-990-0700

• Rochester Public Library
  Business and Social Sciences
    Division
  115 South Avenue
  Rochester 14604
  716-428-7328

Staten Island Council on the Arts
One Edgewater Plaza Rm. 311
Staten Island 10305
718-447-4485

• Onondaga County Public Library
  335 Montgomery Street
  Syracuse 13202
  315-473-4491

• White Plains Public Library
  100 Martine Avenue
  White Plains 10601
  914-682-4488

NORTH CAROLINA

• The Duke Endowment
  200 S. Tryon Street, Ste. 1100
  Charlotte 28202
  704-376-0291

Durham County Library
300 N. Roxboro Street
Durham 27701
919-683-2626

• North Carolina State Library
  109 East Jones Street
  Raleigh 27611
  919-733-3270

• The Winston-Salem Foundation
  229 First Union National Bank
    Building
  Winston-Salem 27101
  919-725-2382

NORTH DAKOTA

Western Dakota Grants Resource
  Center
Bismarck Junior College Library
Bismarck 58501
701-224-5450

• The Library
  North Dakota State University
  Fargo 58105
  701-237-8876

OHIO

• Public Library of Cincinnati
  and Hamilton County
  Education Department
  800 Vine Street
  Cincinnati 45202
  513-369-6940

• The Public Library
  of Columbus and
  Franklin County
  28 S. Hamilton Road
  Columbus 43213-2097
  614-222-7180

Dayton and Montgomery County
  Public Library
Social Sciences Department
215 E. Third Street
Dayton 45402
513-224-1651

Lima–Allen County Regional
  Planning Commission
212 N. Elizabeth Street
Lima 45801
419-228-1836

• Toledo–Lucas County Public
  Library
  Social Science Department
  325 Michigan Street
  Toledo 43624
  419-255-7055 ext.221

Ohio University–Zanesville
  Community Education and
  Development
1425 Newark Road
Zanesville 43701
614-453-0762

OKLAHOMA

• Oklahoma City University Library
  NW 23rd at North Blackwelder
  Oklahoma City 73106
  405-521-5072

• The Support Center
  525 NW Thirteenth Street
  Oklahoma City 73103
  405-236-8133

• Tulsa City–County Library
  System
  400 Civic Center
  Tulsa 74103
  918-592-7944

OREGON

• Library Association of Portland
  Government Documents Room
  801 S.W. Tenth Avenue
  Portland 97205
  503-223-7201

Oregon State Library
State Library Building
Salem 97310
503-378-4243

PENNSYLVANIA

Northampton County Area
  Community College
Learning Resources Center
3835 Green Pond Road
Bethlehem 18017
215-865-5358

• Erie County Public Library
  3 South Perry Square
  Erie 16501
  814-452-2333 ext.54

• Dauphin County Library System
  Central Library
  101 Walnut Street
  Harrisburg 17101
  717-234-4961

Lancaster County Public Library
125 North Duke Street
Lancaster 17602
717-394-2651

• The Free Library of Philadelphia
  Logan Square
  Philadelphia 19103
  215-686-5423

• Hillman Library
  University of Pittsburgh
  Pittsburgh 15260
  412-624-4423

• Economic Development Council of
  Northeastern Pennsylvania
  1151 Oak Street
  Pittston 18640
  717-655-5581

James V. Brown Library
12 E. 4th Street
Williamsport 17701
717-326-0536

RHODE ISLAND

• Providence Public Library
  Reference Department
  150 Empire Street
  Providence 02903
  401-521-7722

SOUTH CAROLINA

• Charleston County Public Library
  404 King Street
  Charleston 29403
  803-723-1645

• South Carolina State Library
  Reader Services Department
  1500 Senate Street
  Columbia 29201
  803-758-3138

SOUTH DAKOTA

• South Dakota State Library
  State Library Building
  800 North Illinois Street
  Pierre 57501
  605-773-3131

Sioux Falls Area Foundation
404 Boyce Greeley Building
321 South Phillips Avenue
Sioux Falls 57102-0781
605-336-7055

TENNESSEE

• Knoxville–Knox County
  Public Library
  500 West Church Avenue
  Knoxville 37902
  615-523-0781

• Memphis Shelby County
  Public Library
  1850 Peabody Avenue
  Memphis 38104
  901-725-8876

• Public Library of Nashville and
  Davidson County
  8th Avenue, North and Union Street
  Nashville 37203
  615-244-4700

TEXAS

Amarillo Area Foundation
1000 Polk
P. O. Box 25569
Amarillo 79105-269
806-376-4521

- **The Hogg Foundation for Mental Health**
  The University of Texas
  Austin 78712
  512-471-5041

- **Corpus Christi State University Library**
  6300 Ocean Drive
  Corpus Christi 78412
  512-991-6810

- **El Paso Community Foundation**
  El Paso National Bank Building
  Suite 1616
  El Paso 79901
  915-533-4020

- **Funding Information Center**
  Texas Christian University Library
  Ft. Worth 76129
  817-921-7664

- **Houston Public Library**
  Bibliographic & Information Center
  500 McKinney Avenue
  Houston 77002
  713-224-5441 ext. 265

- **Funding Information Library**
  507 Brooklyn
  San Antonio 78215
  512-227-4333

- **Dallas Public Library**
  Grants Information Service
  1515 Young Street
  Dallas 75201
  214-749-4100

- **Pan American University**
  Learning Resource Center
  1201 W. University Drive
  Edinburg 78539
  512-381-3304

UTAH

- **Salt Lake City Public Library**
  Business and Science Department
  209 East Fifth South
  Salt Lake City 84111
  801-363-5733

VERMONT

- **State of Vermont Department of Libraries**
  Reference Services Unit
  111 State Street
  Montpelier 05602
  802-828-3261

VIRGINIA

- **Grants Resources Library**
  Hampton City Hall
  22 Lincoln Street, Ninth Floor
  Hampton 23669
  804-727-6496

- **Richmond Public Library**
  Business, Science, & Technology Department
  101 East Franklin Street
  Richmond 23219
  804-780-8223

WASHINGTON

- **Seattle Public Library**
  1000 Fourth Avenue
  Seattle 98104
  206-625-4881

- **Spokane Public Library**
  Funding Information Center
  West 906 Main Avenue
  Spokane 99201
  509-838-3361

WEST VIRGINIA

- **Kanawha County Public Library**
  123 Capital Street
  Charleston 25301
  304-343-4646

WISCONSIN

- **Marquette University Memorial Library**
  1415 West Wisconsin Avenue
  Milwaukee 53233
  414-224-1515

- **University of Wisconsin–Madison**
  Memorial Library
  728 State Street
  Madison 53706
  608-262-3647

  Society for Nonprofit Organizations
  6314 Odana Road
  Suite One
  Madison 53719
  608-274-9777

WYOMING

- **Laramie County Community College Library**
  1400 East College Drive
  Cheyenne 82007
  307-634-5853

CANADA

Canadian Center for Philanthropy
3080 Yonge Street
Suite 4080
Toronto, Ontario M4N3N1
416-484-4118

ENGLAND

Charities Aid Foundation
14 Bloomsbury Square
London WC1A 2LP
01-430-1798

MARIANNA ISLANDS

Northern Marianas College
P.O. Box 1250 CK
Saipan, GM 96950

MEXICO

Biblioteca Benjamin Franklin
Londres 16
Mexico City 6, D.F.
525-591-0244

PUERTO RICO

Universidad Del Sagrado Corazon
M.M.T. Guevarra Library
Correo Calle Loiza
Santurce 00914
809-728-1515 ext. 274

VIRGIN ISLANDS

College of the Virgin Islands Library
Saint Thomas
U.S. Virgin Islands 00801
809-774-9200 ext. 487

THE FOUNDATION CENTER AFFILIATES PROGRAM

Affiliates are libraries or nonprofit agencies that provide fundraising information or other funding-related technical assistance in their communities. Affiliates agree to provide free public access to a basic collection of Foundation Center publications during a regular schedule of hours, offering free funding research guidance to all visitors. Many also provide a variety of special services for local nonprofit organizations using staff or volunteers to prepare special materials, organize workshops, or conduct library orientations.

The affiliates program began in 1981 to continue the expansion of The Foundation Center's funding information network of 90 funding information collections. Since its inception, over 50 organizations have been designated Foundation Center affiliates. Affiliate collections have been established in a wide variety of host organizations, including public and university libraries, technical assistance agencies, and community foundations. The Center maintains strong ties with its affiliates through regular news bulletins, the provision of supporting materials, the sponsorship of regional meetings, and by referring the many nonprofits that call or write to The Foundation Center to the affiliate nearest them.

How to Become a Foundation Center Affiliate Collection

The Foundation Center welcomes inquiries from agencies interested in providing this type of public information service. If you are interested in establishing a funding information library for the use of nonprofit agencies in your area or in learning more about the program, we would like to hear from you.

The first step is for the director of your organization to write to Zeke Kilbride, Network Coordinator, explaining why the collection is needed and how the responsibilities of network participation would be met. The Center will contact you to review the details of the relationship. If your agency is designated an affiliate, you will then be entitled to purchase a core collection of Foundation Center materials at a 20% discount rate (annual cost of approx. $370). Center staff will be happy to assist in identifying supplementary titles for funding information libraries and can arrange for the purchase and monthly shipment from the Internal Revenue Service of private foundation tax returns on microfiche. A core collection, which must be maintained from year to year, consists of current editions of the following publications:

The Foundation Directory
The Foundation Directory Supplement
The Foundation Grants Index
The Foundation Grants Index Bimonthly
Source Book Profiles
The National Data Book
Foundation Fundamentals

For more information, please write to: Zeke Kilbride, The Foundation Center, 79 Fifth Avenue, New York, NY 10003.

8/86

Bibliography for Proposal Writers

(Prices are not necessarily current. Some books are out of print, but use them at your library or at one of the Foundation Center cooperating collections listed on pp. 76-79.)

Sources of funds

General

Annual Register of Grant Support. Chicago: Marquis Academic Media ($69.50). Provides detailed information on grant programs of government agencies, public and private foundations, corporations, community trusts, unions, educational and professional associations, and special interest organizations. Includes eligibility information. Cataloged by fields of interest.

ARIS Funding Messenger. San Francisco: Academic Research Information System (3 sections, each published monthly: *Social & Natural Sciences Report,* $135/year; *Creative Arts & Humanities Report,* $135/year; *Medical Sciences Report,* $75/year; complete, $295/year). Provides information in some detail on federal, foundation, and corporate funding programs. Lists many opportunities of interest to faculty with research projects, including corporate requests for new products and technologies.

Foundations

The Foundation Center Source Book Profiles. New York: The Foundation Center (subscription to approximately 500 profiles, $265/year). Analytical profiles of the 1,000 largest foundations (including 150 company-sponsored and 25 community foundations) that do not restrict funds programmatically. Includes list of sample grants. Subscription includes *Foundation Profile Updates,* a bimonthly news service that highlights changes and gives new cumulative indexes. Free sample profile available.

The Foundation Directory. New York: The Foundation Center ($60). *Foundation Directory Supplement* ($30). Descriptive information on over 4,000 of the largest foundations in the U.S. Arranged alphabetically by state, indexed by program area and by individual administrators, donors, and trustees.

The Foundation Grants Index Annual. New York: The Foundation Center (annual vol., $40; updates in *The Foundation Grants Index Bimonthly,* $20/year). Reviews patterns of giving for about 500 foundations. Lists grants of $5,000 or more awarded to nonprofit organizations during preceding year. Includes recipient name and geographic location, amount and date of grant, and grant purpose. Helpful because foundations do not publish current lists of available funds. Indexed by recipient and subject.

Freeman, David F. *The Handbook on Private Foundations.* Washington, DC: Council on Foundations, 1981 ($14.95). A "how-to" guide from the foundation viewpoint. Discusses grant-making philosophy, handling and evaluating grant requests, processing applications, and IRS codes and regulations.

Lawson, David M. *Foundation 500—An Index to Foundation Giving Patterns.* New York: Douglas M. Lawson Associates, 1979 (now out-of-print; may be available at a library). Desk-top research guide to programs and geographical distribution of 500 of the nation's top foundations. Indexed by subject, geographic recipient, and dollar amount of grants. Includes a section analyzing current trends in the distribution of grants by subject and geographical location. Mainly historic interest.

National Data Book. New York: The Foundation Center (2 vols., published annually, $55). Source for smaller foundations. Includes information on the more than 22,000 nonprofit organizations classified as private U.S. foundations. Provides a brief profile of each, culled primarily from IRS returns. Indexed alphabetically and by state; no subject index.

State directories of foundations. Usually published by the Secretary of State's office. Range in price from $5 to $25. Some updated annually, some every five to 10 years. Connecticut, Massachusetts, Illinois, Minnesota directories available, among others.

Taft Foundation Reporter, 12 issues *Foundation Giving Watch/Updates.* Washington, DC: The Taft Corporation (*Directory,* $267; *Updates,* 12 issues, $110; if *Directory* and *Updates* purchased together, $347/year; discount when purchased with *Taft Corporate Directory* and *Profiles*). Gives detailed information on 500 private foundations, including biographies of directors and trustees. Monthly newsletter includes eight-page update on giving trends and specific foundations.

Corporations and corporate foundations

Chicago Corporate Connection. Chicago: Donors Forum of Chicago, 1983 ($15). Giving guidelines of 200 Chicago area corporations. Contains information that is not available elsewhere on some corporations without formal programs. No list of grants.

Corporate 500: The Directory of Corporate Philanthropy. San Francisco: Public Management Institute, 1984 ($245 plus shipping).

Corporate Foundation Profiles. New York: The Foundation Center, 1983 (512 pp., $50). Contains three- to six-page detailed analyses of more than 200 of the largest company-sponsored foundations with full subject, support type, and geographic indices. Includes brief financial data for more than 300 smaller corporate foundations.

Taft Corporate Directory, 12 issues *Corporate Giving Watch/Profiles.* Washington, DC: The Taft Corporation (*Directory,* $267; *Profiles,* 12 issues, $127; discount if *Directory* and *Profiles* purchased together, $347/year; discount if purchased with *Taft Foundation Reporter* and *Updates*). *Directory* contains 400 detailed profiles, including 50 direct giving reports. Includes biographies of corporate directors, who are also indexed by alma mater. Monthly newsletter includes eight- to 10-page update on corporations and trends in corporate giving.

Proposal development and writing

General

A Manual of Style. Chicago: The University of Chicago Press, 1969 ($20). An exhaustively complete work covering all aspects of producing printed matter, including manuscript preparation, style, and design and typography.

Fowler, H. W. *A Dictionary of Modern English Usage.* 2nd ed. Oxford: Clarendon Press, 1983 ($8.95). A basic tool for all writers. The examples are especially helpful.

Strunk, William, Jr., and White, E. B. *The Elements of Style.* New York: Macmillan, 1979 ($6.95; paperback, $2.25). An indispensable guide, concise yet thorough, to elementary English usage, composition, and stylistic considerations.

Zinsser, William. *On Writing Well: An Informal Guide to Writing Nonfiction.* 3rd ed. New York: Harper & Row, 1985 (paperback, $8.95). A good companion to Strunk and White. Aimed generally at journalists and other expository writers, but advice on style appropriate for proposals as well.

Development

Abeles, Fred B. "How to Prepare an Effective Scientific Research Proposal." *The Grantsmanship Center News.* Jan./Feb. 1982, pp. 52-57. Covers the writing of a scientific research proposal, including a section on relevant issues in formulating the research project itself.

Decker, Virginia A., and Decker, Larry E. *The Funding Process: Grantsmanship and Proposal Development.* Charlottesville, VA: Community Collaborators, 1978 ($6.95). Outlines each phase of grantsmanship process: idea development, funding source identification, proposal writing and submission, review procedure, and grant administration. Appended: locations of information centers.

Dermer, Joseph. *How to Write Successful Foundation Presentations.* Hartsdale, NY: Public Service Materials Center, 1977 ($9.95). A painstaking guide to a full range of proposal writing applications, ranging from the appointment letter to special project presentations to letters of renewal. Includes sample forms for each type of proposal or letter.

Gayley, Henry T. *How to Write for Development.* Washington, DC: Council for Advancement and Support of Education, 1981 ($16.50). A general overview of writing for development purposes, aimed specifically at uses for higher education. The basic principles, however, are applicable to any field.

Grantsmanship: Money and How to Get It. 2nd ed. Chicago: Marquis Academic Media, 1978 ($7.50). Suggests how to define goals, locate donors, prepare proposals, and report results.

Hall, Mary. *Developing Skills in Proposal Writing.* 2nd ed. Portland, OR: Continuing Education, 1977. A general guide covering methods for pre-proposal planning as well as the writing, review, and submission of the proposal itself.

Hillman, Howard, and Abarbanel, Karin. *The Art of Winning Foundation Grants.* New York: Vanguard, 1975 ($8.95). Step-by-step guide to the development and writing of grant proposals.

Kiritz, Norton J. *Program Planning and Proposal Writing.* Expanded version. Los Angeles: The Grantsmanship Center, 1980. A planning and writing guide covering in detail each section of the proposal, from the initial summary to the formulation of the budget.

Kurzig, Carol. *Foundation Fundamentals: A Resource Guide for Grantseekers.* 3rd ed. New York: The Foundation Center, 1985 ($9.95). Describes how to identify funding sources by subject area or geographic origin. Provides proposal checklists and worksheets. Extensive bibliography.

Teague, Gerald V., and Heathington, Betty S. *The Process of Grant Proposal Development.* Bloomington, IN: Phi Delta Kappa Educational Foundation, 1980 ($.75). Step-by-step guide to developing a grant application for educational project funding. Reviews grant terminology, funding sources, proposal development, review process, agency contacts, etc.

General information

Books

Lamaire, Ingrid. *Resource Directory for Funding and Managing of Non-profit Organizations.* New York: The Edna McConnell Clark Foundation, 1977. Covers all aspects of resource development, including management support for nonprofit organizations.

Periodicals

Foundation News: The Magazine of Philanthropy (bimonthly, $24). Council on Foundations, Inc., 1828 L St. NW, Washington, DC 20036. Aims to increase public understanding of the role of philanthropy. Provides a forum for communication between organizations and individuals in the field.

Fund Raising Management (monthly magazine, $4; $36/yr). 224 Seventh St., Garden City, NY 11530. Information on general fund-raising techniques, relating to all areas and disciplines.

Grants Magazine: The Journal of Sponsored Research and Other Programs (quarterly; individuals, $27; institutions, $54). Plenum Publishing Corporation, 227 West 17th St., New York, NY 10011. Interdisciplinary forum for issues affecting public and private philanthropy. Includes section called "Grants Clinic," which examines successful grant proposals.

The Grantsmanship Center News (bimonthly, $20). 1015 West Olympic Blvd., Los Angeles, CA 90015. Source for "how-to" information on federal and foundation funding. Contains feature articles, "funding notes" and "deadlines" columns, and book reviews.

Other research tools

External sources

Dun & Bradstreet:
  Million Dollar Directory
  Reference Book of Corporate Managements
  Monthly Supplement

Moody's:
  Industrial Manual
  OTC
  Bank & Finance

Securities and Exchange Commission:
  Official Summary
  Monthly Updates

Standard & Poor's Directories:
    Index
    Register of Corporations, Directors and Executives
    Corporations

Directory of Corporate Affiliations
Directory of Advertising Agencies
Directory of Advertisers
A.G. Becker Guide
Master Biographical Index
Who's Who Publications
Martindale & Hubbell Law Directory
American Men & Women of Science
Directory of American Scholars
Congressional Directory and *Congressional Staff Directory*
Social registers
Rand McNally International Bankers Directory
Barron's National Business and Financial Weekly
New York Times
Wall Street Journal
Forbes, Business Week, Fortune
"Local" magazines, such as *Connecticut, New York, Chicago*
Corporate and foundation annual reports
Proxy statements
Quarterly reports
Local histories
Theater, concert programs
Membership lists
Other colleges' annual reports

Internal sources

Trustee lists and surveys
Roster of graduates' employment (also spouses, parents)
Matching gift list by corporation and individual
List of recruiters
Department annual reports
Department surveys of graduates
Alumni magazines, newsletters
Past and current list of student enrollments by course, department, and major
Donor lists
Yearbooks
Attendance lists

Organizations

Council on Foundations, Inc.
1828 L St. NW
Washington, DC 20036

Donor's Forum of Chicago
208 South LaSalle St.
Chicago, IL 60604

The Foundation Center
Home offices:
79 Fifth Ave.
New York, NY 10003
and 1001 Connecticut Ave., Suite 936
Washington, DC 20036

The Grantsmanship Center
1031 South Grand Ave.
Los Angeles, CA 90015